Value Branding with Social Media Marketing

Jaw-Dropping Secrets for Facebook Ads, YouTube, Instagram, Twitter for Over
One Million Followers and 10000 Dollar Monthly Cash Flow

Casey Greenwood

Legal Notice

This book is copyright protected. This book is only for personal use. You cannot amend, distribute, sell, use, quote or paraphrase any part, or the content within this book, without the consent of the author or publisher.

Disclaimer Notice

Please note the information contained within this document is for educational and entertainment purposes only. All effort has been executed to present accurate, up to date, and reliable, complete information. No warranties of any kind are declared or implied. Readers acknowledge that the author is not engaging in the rendering of legal, financial, medical or professional advice. The content within this book has been derived from various sources. Please consult a licensed professional before attempting any techniques outlined in this book.

By reading this document, the reader agrees that under no circumstances is the author responsible for any losses, direct or indirect, which are incurred as a result of the use of information contained within this document, including, but not limited to, — errors, omissions, or inaccuracies.

Contents

Chapter 1:
Social Media Marketing is Now a Requirement

There are hundreds and hundreds of millions of people on social media. That's a massive amount of people to try to imagine. Social media is a global phenomenon that has changed how the world operates. What used to be impossible is now a task completed with a few simple buttons. There are more people online every day than there has been ever before. Social media is growing at a rapid rate, and it's not slowing down anytime soon. Before we know it, we'll likely be handed a cell phone at birth, never getting the chance to escape the online world.

Here's the best part. You can profit from those numbers and find ways to grow your business. What used to have to take ad campaigns, and days of deals to establish a prime spot can now be done all on our social media pages. To advertise a decade ago, you might have looked to your local paper, or maybe you could afford a spot on your local news channel. Now, you can make a post right where you're sitting, exposing your brand and product to the hundreds of millions of people that get online every day.

People not only want more content, but they're hungry for it. Though there are so many people online, finding truly original content can be challenging. A lot of what we see is regurgitated — only thinking on the surface level of what their customers might want. Though people are still using more and more social media every day, that doesn't mean we aren't still desperate for something new. Not everything that's a new idea always works, but when it does get it right, it explodes. Once a trend is discovered online, there's a trickle effect on other brands to follow suit. Social media allows anyone to have that effect, to be the new trend. Now more than ever, social media users are desperate to find ways that they can use social media in an innovative way.

Companies, no matter what their brand or product is, can find ways to benefit from the online world. There are multiple ways that we can find success online, so what might not work at first can be changed to something that brings more success. There are countless audiences out there waiting for our content, our products, and it's our job to find them. Just because we don't at first doesn't mean that we can't at all. There are so many different platforms, and methods of marketing within those social media, that we will always have a new way to try something when the first method might not work out exactly as we planned. If you're a restaurant wanting to reach out to more people, or perhaps a B2B company looking to expand clients, you can feel confident knowing that you'll find success with online marketing through social media. There aren't just benefits in marketing on this larger company scale either. Independents looking to brand themselves will have a lot of success when they start expanding their brand online.

Whether you're a freelancer looking to gain clients, or a model wanting to influence, you can find ways to market yourself and your brand on an individual level. Customers respond well to individuals that sell themselves. We go online to feel more connected to people, and that goes just beyond the friends and family we already know. Following certain celebrities means that you get a peek into their lives, and it allows their followers to make personal connections with them. When you can do the same for your brand, you will have people responding positively while being able to also market your content and products.

The point of using social media marketing is to get people to your website, and from there, they can spend their money on your products, or click on ads for more revenue to your business account. The better you are at understanding what works best in a successful ad campaign, the easier it will be for you to make money. As you grow online, you will start to discover that you can cash in on your brand in more ways than just what your original marketing attempts might have intended.

How Many People Are on The Internet?

The Internet provides many options for those looking for more in their lives. What is dissatisfactory in the real world can be resolved online. It provides an escape, a fantasy, and a glimpse at a life that's different than our own. You can play games, meet new people, and even pretend you're someone you're not. You can go on there for love, for a job, or to connect with family. Whatever your intentions are when you open your phone, tablet, laptop, or even TV, you can be confident that they will be fulfilled. Beyond that, you will discover so much more in the process.

In a world that's so demanding of innovation and money, we tend to get lost with our intentions in this capitalist society. As soon as social media emerged, so did brand marketing within these platforms. Advertisements can sometimes be intrusive on people's lives, and social media engineers have discovered this. Now, it seems to be the attempt of the top social media brands to offer their users a way to experience their app with less organic ads, and content that has more value for those using it. What there seems to be an emphasis on social media more now are interactions that are meaningful to users.

There are over 7.5 billion people in the world, and that's just an estimate on what's recorded combined with an idea of what we can't register. That's a lot of people, and as time goes on, the number keeps growing. Centuries ago, sending a message could take months, years, or sometimes just be downright impossible. The world was more divided, not by differences but by geography and inability to communicate. Social media has bridged those gaps, and now there are endless ways we can communicate with more people globally than ever before.

There are five billion cell phone users, four billion of them being on the Internet. That means, with a collection of the information we know, we can make the rough estimate that half of the people in the world are online. Who could have ever imagined 100, 50, 20 years ago, that we would be able to market our brand to half the people on the planet? We've known about famous people before, and we've seen international trends that changed the world as a whole but knowing that anyone is capable of that if they just get on social media is pretty wild to think about. There aren't any Instagram accounts that are even close to that just yet, but in a few years, who knows who might be the first user to have 1 billion followers?

The Emergence of Social Media

3 billion people in the world use social media, and we can be sure that a large portion of those individuals uses multiple platforms. While you might be able to market your brand in one way on an individual platform reaching thousands of people, you can reach even more individuals on a different platform. And for those that you missed on one account; you might be able to convince to buy into your brand on another. We can incorporate our companies into people's lives and make it easier for them to have access to our trends, brands, products, services, and overall content.

If you could reach just .01 percent of people in the world, you would still be able to reach out to 100,000 individuals. 100,000 to see your post might only result in 1,000 people going to your website, but that's still a return on one free post you made online. You can pay to have your things advertised, but there are also many free options for business users when it comes to using social media to market yourself.

Social media is still growing, as well. Each year, there is about a 7 percent jump in the amount of social media users. As the Internet becomes more accessible to those that don't have it and more necessary for those that already do, we will only see more advancements in the overall services of these platforms. Having social media accounts is a requirement for anyone that wants to have social capital in this world, and before we know it, it will become a requirement for all brands that want to find success as well.

We have to look at the ways our brands are globally relevant as well. You might be a small clothing company in Illinois, but soon, you could become an international company when you find the right market of people across the border and over the oceans. It might not be anything you ever expected, but that doesn't mean it's not totally possible for you and your brand. All we have to do is know how to market ourselves. These accounts have many different algorithms that determine what they will show users, and as a brand that wants to find online success, it's up to you to know how to beat these algorithms.

The Money Put into Social Media

The social media marketing world is a billion-dollar industry. Companies pour millions and millions of dollars into social media marketing, and in return, they either just get a few clicks to their website or customers that make purchases. All the while, platforms like Facebook, YouTube, and Twitter are all cashing in on the clicks as well. The only people that can be certain they're making money from this online marketing strategy are the people on the social media site, not necessarily the brand. It is up to you to make sure that you are creating something marketable, shareable, and clickable so that your business finds the most success through their desired ad campaign.

Most companies have shared that their marketing efforts on social media account for at least twenty percent of their marketing budget. There are many different ways you can market your brand or company. You can take out ads in the paper, on TV, or on billboards. You can buy a magazine spot or find your ad on a regular website. While all of this cost money, remember that many social media marketing strategies can be completely free. All you have to do is know how to post the right thing to get the right kind of attention.

Social networks earn over 8 billion in 2015, and the number will only seem to grow. You can rest assured that social media marketing isn't going anywhere anytime soon. Before we know it, the twenty percent average that goes into social media marketing will become 50, 70, and 100 percent, making other forms of ads obsolete. Don't wait to get on this train. Take advantage of all the things social media marketing has to offer because your competitors already are.

You don't have to spend a single dime on social media marketing either. There are plenty of ways that you can grow your business through organic marketing. This will involve posting anything as you would type on a social or personal account. Without even paying a penny, you can market your brand and sell products using the free tools that everyone else has access to online.

Chapter 2:
The Big 4 Social Media Platforms

There was one platform that we all started on. Perhaps you heard about it from a friend, or you were bored online one day and stumbled upon a website that you could create an account on. It's strange to think that we were born in a time when social media was also created. Our children and their children won't know a time before now, and we will be among the last of the people that do know this feeling. Though bittersweet, it's also something that comes to our advantage.

We're the pioneers of online marketing. We can become a part of the innovations that emerge every day for different brands to market themselves online. Many people switched from one to the next, as well when social media first appeared. Now, however, we know that it's essential for us to get on multiple platforms to make sure our brand is spreading out as much as possible. These all exist for free, so it would almost hurt our image more if we avoided specific methods of marketing to others.

There are all kinds of social media platforms now, and you can find ones specific to your niches. Whether you have a particular hobby, interest, or habit, you can find a community online specific to your needs. As brands, we can identify these niches and find ways to incorporate our own products and services in advertisements catered towards these groups of people. Not only are we targeting just one either, but multiple groups and categories of people that are waiting for brands like ours to change their life for the better.

The average time that people spend on social media is almost 2 hours a day. That gives you 2 hours to try and reach as many people as possible. Of course, they're not going to spend those two hours on your site for watching your videos, but they could. Even if they don't follow you, there are methods you can take to get your brand and videos out there for people to see, multiple different ways, and various times throughout the day.

90 percent of retail outlets use two different social media platforms. This is a reminder that your competitors are likely already doing the same! Now more than ever, we need to put an emphasis on sharing our brands online so that they can reach as many people as possible. There's never been a brand that suffered because they received too much exposure, after all. We're most likely to find the most success when we can reach out to a wide range of specified groups curated through our following. The only way to find those groups is to expose our brand and create awareness so that we can reach as many individuals as possible.

We can estimate that, depending on the platform, there is a new social media user every ten seconds, with some sites having more or less than that amount of new accounts. That means that every ten seconds, you are given a chance to reach out to a unique individual. You have access to so many people that are already online, but second after second, we can find a new user on a different social media platform, and they could become a potential customer. This is an incredible tool that generations before us could never have imagined. It's our time now to take that power and use it for good. So many companies are using lazy marketing tactics and creating brand awareness for things that don't have meaning. With a strong vision, you can break through that clutter and stand out against the many competitors you'll face online.

YouTube

YouTube has 1.5 billion users. It is the second most popular search engine aside from Google, with billions of searches a day. Many people will watch YouTube not logged in as well, so the number of users on it daily can sometimes be even more significant. YouTube started as just a place to share videos. No one ever could have imagined that it would become as relevant as cable television. Who would have thought that this video platform would have a tutorial for how to do just about anything in a few decades? It's hard to find a website that doesn't have a link to their YouTube video somewhere on the page. Many people can admit they've gotten lost in more than one YouTube hole, endlessly clicking on more related videos until we got lost in a strange video, we never intended on seeing in the first place.

Over 1 billion YouTube hours are watched every day. YouTube is viewed in bed, on the toilet, at work, on the bus. It's on your television, in your hand, and everywhere else you look. If there's a screen, it's likely played a YouTube video at one point or another. Most people have a YouTube page, even if they aren't posting videos themselves. Some old things might be surfacing the internet we regret, and other things we might be hoping hits 1,000,000 views. YouTube is ubiquitous, and it's a tool that can help us grow ourselves and our businesses.

95 percent of the internet population has access to YouTube, meaning very few international locations won't be able to see specific content. YouTube has subtitles, and many videos are offered in multiple languages. YouTube videos don't need dialogue either, and people are finding ways to communicate their messages without having to use their spoken language to make their point. This has allowed people to have an international reach to new users that might have never found their products without the use of social media.

94 percent of 18-24-year old's also use YouTube. This is the target audience that we should really focus on hitting. Even if you're selling products like baby toys or adult diapers, these people might still have the purchasing power over these products, so a group this broad is

essential to consider hitting. Most of us will have products or brands that are for this age gap, which puts us at an even more significant advantage.

Facebook

Facebook tops the charts with 2.271 billion users. Facebook started with simple hope to connect the elite Ivy League, college members. Now, it's a place where you can see someone post a birth announcement, rant about their work, or share a video of a funny cat. Facebook has so many opportunities to connect individuals that might otherwise have gone their entire lives without knowing about the other. It's a place where you can add your long-distance friends and keep updated with their lives. You can learn about local concerts happening in your area and "like" the restaurants that you frequent. The movies you enjoy watching can post updates, and your favorite celebrities can share status updates. It's much more than a form of communication. It's a tool we can use for our brands and companies.

The average Facebook user will spend at least 35 minutes on Facebook a day. This is an average as well, with some users spending just a few minutes, and others spending up to hours on Facebook. Through all these minutes of liking, sharing, and commenting, there are opportunities for brands to spread their mission statements and connect to users that are hungry for new media. Facebook gives us the chance to tap into a world that can help us expand our horizons and articulate the goals created behind our brand.

There are 6 new profiles created every second. That is six chances for your brand a second to become exposed to a new user. When you can find methods of combining brand awareness and product selling through organic and paid advertising, you have mastered how to reach out to most individuals that will come across your company's page.

Out of all the logins that occur on a particular brand's website, fifty percent of their site traffic comes from Facebook. This means that when a site gets 1,000 visitors in one day, around five hundred, give or take a few, will have arrived there through Facebook! This proves that brands that are not on Facebook could be losing as much as double their current site traffic! It's more important now than ever that we put ourselves out there on Facebook.

Instagram

Instagram has 1 billion users. It's no surprise to know that Facebook is actually the owner of Instagram, after shelling out over six digits for the up and coming website. There are ways that you can combine your profiles through both apps, or you can use them independently of each other. The most important thing to remember, however, is that Instagram can be just as important as Facebook, if not more, depending on your brand. There are individual companies that will do better on Instagram than they might on Facebook. A big part of this is because of the different kinds of followers that appear within each app.

4.2 billion likes will go out to various pictures every single day. These are spread between millions of images but imagine seeing 4.2 billion hearts appear on your screen! That's how many times people are tapping their phones to send a little heart out to the people that they're following. Those hearts go out to people who post pictures of themselves, their families, and the food that they're eating. The center is sent through love, letting the other person know they're supported. The heart is thrown when something is funny and gives the viewer a laugh. The center is given to an animal that's cute and doesn't even know that it's getting so many likes on social media.

71 percent of Americans are on Instagram. This means that by putting your brand on Instagram, you're opening your company to 7 out of 10 people in America. Marketing like this is enormous. You used to have to pay a lot of money to get that kind of exposure. Sometimes, even putting your ad on during a sure popular TV show couldn't get you that much exposure. We have that power all on our own now, however, and it can happen any time you want.

1 in 4 teens will state that Instagram is their favorite platform. Out of the other three teens, they might not be on any social media at all, meaning that Instagram is essential for those that are going to be targeting the youth of our world. More people get on the app every day, so it doesn't seem like new users will be slowing down any time soon.

Twitter

Twitter is still very much active with 326 million users. It's been around longer than some apps and not as popular as others, but it is still very relevant, especially in the marketing world. Twitter is important because it's a way that communication has opened up between different brands and their followers. By allowing such a great way to interact with companies, Twitter users feel more confident with their purchases knowing that they have a voice that's been heard. This is how social media has helped us brand ourselves not only more comfortable but for the better.

500 million visits occur to Twitter every month from users that aren't even logged in. This means that of those hundreds of millions of users, you also have a chance to reach millions more each day that doesn't have a Twitter at all! Since statistics like these are high for Twitter, we can assume that they are for other sites as well. Though it is better to reach out to a follower who can become loyal, brand awareness is still crucial for getting new leads and people interested in your products and content.

45 percent of Americans are on Twitter. At least four out of 10 of the people you meet will have a Twitter. They could potentially be the three that don't have an Instagram as well! Though there will always be people that don't have social media accounts, you can still get as many people on board with your brand when you use multiple platforms.

77 people on Twitter state that they have a better perspective on the businesses they like when they interact with that company. That is proof enough that your company will find success when you start sending out tweets and favoriting the words that others decide to use. When you can reply to a customer or respond to a fan, they feel even more connected to you than they did when they initially followed, and this will help them build loyalty to your brand.

Which One You Should Choose

When looking at statistics as necessary as these, you might start to think to yourself which one you should pick. It can be easy to say that you'll get on Facebook first because it has the most users. However, just because this is true, that doesn't mean you'll find as much success. Think about it in terms of opening an actual business. You could think opening your restaurant on a busy street in New York is better than a small town in the Midwest because obviously, the population is higher. However, you're also putting yourself up against other competitors, and you also are at risk of hitting the wrong group of people as well. Just because one app has more users doesn't mean that it should be the only one you use.

The answer is that you should choose all of them. You will likely benefit from having just one social media account, but if you find ways to include all of them, you're only opening yourself up to more exposure. You don't want to post on all of them always, because too much content can be a bad thing if not handled correctly. What's important to do, however, is to determine ways that you can incorporate these platforms all together to make one cohesive image for your brand.

First and foremost, select the place that has the most users relevant to your products. If you're a beauty company that sells natural makeup products, Instagram might be your first choice because you'll be able to hit up beauty vloggers and tap into their following. After that, you can then decide to expand to the others. You don't have to open all social media accounts at once. In fact, you might find that you become overwhelmed if you do this. If you're running your marketing strategy alone, it might be best to start with just one type of social media. After that, you can grow your brand and spread to others.

You might even find that you get more followers when you do this because you can advertise one social media page on a different account. For example, you might start an Instagram, gain a following of 10,000, and then decide to move to Facebook. If you had just gone to Facebook in the first place, you would have a certain number of followers, but you could gain more by promoting the opening of your Facebook page on your Instagram.

Even if your platform has a small amount of your type of user, then you will still be able to reach out to that audience. When you work closely with your audiences, you can expect a higher rate of the turnaround. You could hit 100,000 viewers on an ad for your product, but if your brand is only relevant to 1,000 of them, then you won't get as many sales.

On the other hand, if you targeted a group of just 20,000 that are specifically chosen for your product, then you might get a higher rate of return on your product even though it was seen by fewer people. Choose the right platforms for your brand first, and then grow your image to be inclusive of them all.

Chapter 3:
Why YouTube is the Leading Platform

YouTube is seemingly becoming the new way that people consume their content. Out of the last few things you've seen, how many have been on YouTube? You might realize that you only watch a few hours of YouTube a week versus how many combined hours of TV and movies you see, but it might actually end up being closer to the same amount. YouTube feels like we consume it less because it's given to us in smaller doses, but billions of minutes of YouTube videos are still being watched day after day, so it shows in the numbers that we are watching way more YouTube than what we might think.

We covered a lot of vital statistics in the last chapter. It's easy to see that reaching teens is essential in marketing, and almost all teens are on YouTube. Though all teens might not have YouTube accounts, it is still the way that they are watching their media. Some teens have even stated that they use live streams to watch movies that aren't available on other streaming services! Though this isn't the kind of behavior that should be applauded, we still need to be realistic in understanding that using YouTube can be a very successful way to reach our youth.

Still, older users are on the app as well, with half of the Internet users over 75 years old are also on YouTube. YouTube isn't just a place where you can watch funny videos or music videos. You can see entire documentaries, how-to instructional, and simply vlogs checking in with other people. It's another platform in which we can communicate with others, on YouTube, it's just in a different way.

Out of those YouTube users, there is only about 15 percent that is in the U.S. While you can still assume that millions of users are still in the U.S., places like India have almost as many users on the platform as well. Since YouTube is global, we can reach more than just U.S. followers when it comes to the content that we are creating.

The Importance of YouTube

YouTube is integrated into our lives, with at least a fourth of users being on the app on their phones. If you're standing at the kitchen counter trying to figure out how to tell if an egg is still good, or if you should preheat the oven to 350 or 400 degrees, you might decide to pull out your phone and look it up on YouTube. If you're standing behind the bathroom sink with a wrench trying to figure out why your faucet isn't working, you might go on YouTube. If you're bored on the couch with a bag full of makeup and want to experiment with your look, you might go on YouTube. It's clear to see that you are going to find what you need by opening up this app, and if we didn't have it, many people would likely find themselves at a disadvantage.

YouTube is essential for music users, those looking for relaxation videos, and videos that teach their viewers something. These are among some of the highest-ranking videos on YouTube right now. The top viewed videos are all ones that belong to different musicians as well, with the most views going out to their official videos. Aside from those types of videos, the ones that do really well are also inclusive of relaxing videos or ones that are instructional.

Gaming and reviews are also critical on YouTube. If an individual creates an account to play video games or to review products, they will often find a lot of people going to their channel to get their sense for whether or not they too should buy into that brand.

People want new content, and they want something substantial, that's more than just a social media post. Not many people are still signing up for cable, so with the emergence of other apps like Netflix and Hulu, it's clear to see that this is another excellent streaming service to give people the content they want.

How to Start

You'll first want to start by making a profile for your brand or business and decide how you're going to incorporate your brand. Your YouTube name should be something similar to what your other social media names might be. It might not be the exact thing, and that username might already be taken, but you still want it to be something that can quickly identify you to your other viewers and followers that are on different platforms. If you make your YouTube profile difficult for your other followers to find, then you are only putting yourself at a disadvantage.

Once your profile is complete, you should get started by liking and following videos and accounts relevant to your brand. First and foremost, you're going to want to develop your competitors. It might sound counterintuitive, but this is going to be the way to get you in on your target audience. After a while, you don't have to follow them, but it will get your feed and your algorithm aligned with the content that you're going to be putting out there.

Now, it will be time for you to get the videos ready that you want to upload. It will be up to you to decide what kind of videos you are going to be uploading. You can create videos that are strictly advertisements that exist for brand awareness. You might also want to put a twist on your company and create interesting videos that attract more than just people that want to buy your product. For example, if you're a real estate investor, you could do house tours, or maybe even vlog a renovation project. If you're a beauty blogger, makeup tutorials are incredibly popular. If you own a restaurant, you could do a tour, a little documentary, and even share recipes and make instructional cooking videos. YouTube will allow you to be very fluid with the kind of content you want to post, so that part will be up to you.

When it comes time to upload, one trick is to comment on a related video that you are posting something similar to and share a comment that you're going to release new content. For example, if you are going to be posting a video on how to gain 100,000 followers on Instagram overnight, then you'll want to first search that same title in your own browser. Then, you can go to that video and post a comment saying something about how you're going to post your first video, and simply create awareness for yourself in a place that you can find your right audience. You might realize that you can gain as many followers as 1,000 before you even post your first video if you are using this trick.

You will then want to make sure that you are appropriately labeling and tagging your videos, so they reach the right people. We will get into further tagging and labeling in the next chapter, but it's important to remember this in your posting process. There are going to be trial and error periods, and we're going to cover those in the next section, along with tips to see how you can really expand your company.

How You Can Grow on YouTube

The best way to make sure you grow is to interact and post consistently new content. People are going to want to rely on you for new content. Places that post videos every weekly, and at specific times, like Mondays at 7 P.M., are going to have the most subscribers because they've given their fans a dedicated time that they can be counted on. Some people are creatures of habit, and others just want to know that they always have new content that they can rely on.

Your YouTube videos will evolve, and that's a good thing. You can find more ways to incorporate new ideas to keep your content new and fresh. If you look at any successful YouTube page, the first video they posted is going to be way different from the most recent thing that they shared. It's important to remember that your first YouTube video isn't going to be perfect, so don't put this kind of pressure on yourself. Just do your best to make something interesting, unique, and consumable each and every time, and you'll be sure to find your success.

Before you get started, make sure that you are studying the brands that are similar to yours, and who your competitors might be. The more research you do in preparation for your channel launching, the better you will be able to have an idea of what works and what doesn't. While you want to make sure that you're not copying anything that your competitors are doing, it's still crucial that you are aware of making sure that you aren't missing any tricks or doing something that seemingly doesn't actually work.

Remember to keep track of those that could become potential collaborators down the line as well. When you can link up with other YouTubes of similar categories, you will find more success than if you just try to do it all alone, as a solo YouTuber.

Finding Success on YouTube

Not as many people will find success on YouTube as they might hope, but it is possible. Some individuals can grow their following overnight, and there will be other users that it might take years to go from 0 to 10,000. Whatever your pace might be, don't let it be something that discourages you. Though you might be hopeful for speedy results, be prepared that it could take a little bit to get off the ground. Remember, the more you grow, however, the higher your rate of growth will be. For example, if you grow 1,000 followers in one week, then the next week, your chances of developing more are higher since you have more followers to share your content. You just have to know when to keep going and know when to try something new. Some videos might just need more time to reach different audiences, and some videos might not be working at all.

YouTube success doesn't happen overnight, either. If you go to the top pages, some might have posted for a couple of years before they found real fame. When you can find success, it's going to be something that you carry with you for a while. If you're putting out content that people like, then you'll have consistent followers. You can keep up with what people are saying about your channel as well so that you can improve it for the better. Eventually, YouTube can become a passive form of income. If a video continues to get 100,000 views or more every year, ultimately, your video will have hit a million views and all the while, you might have made money from that.

Common Mistakes

The biggest mistake new users make is by using bait. There are a lot of things on YouTube that tells viewers, "click here to see this crazy thing that happened." Understanding customers, "find instant success with this video," is a way to get people to click rapidly, but more often than not, they won't find that instant success and will get discouraged. Getting a lot of views might seem reasonable at first, but if people aren't satisfied, then they will give it a thumb down and eventually YouTube won't suggest it anymore. If you use an image as your thumbnail that isn't even in the video, then it will make people annoyed, and they won't go back to your other videos. There is some slight inflation of words in the title that can help, but you shouldn't always rely on something shocking to get people to click on your video.

They also shouldn't try to change things up too much. Some YouTubers will gain a decent following and then try to change things up once they hit the next plateau. Some will keep changing in the hopes that they will keep getting new followers every time. While change is good, make sure that it still aligns with your brand, and you're not just using it as a bait tactic for new followers.

Branding yourself using only other people are going to make it harder for you to stick out as well. Some people will copy someone else's headlines exactly, and there are specific individuals that will try to dress and talk like the most popular YouTube stars as well. While it can be helpful sometimes to mention or include other popular YouTubers or their styles in your videos, you still have to make sure that your brand is sticking out from others and that you're not getting lost in another YouTuber's aesthetic.

Chapter 4:
Hacking the YouTube Algorithm

This chapter is going to be a little longer than the rest because we really want to emphasize the importance of YouTube. At the same time, the tips we give for these videos will also apply to the videos that you'll be making for Facebook, Twitter, and Instagram as well. YouTube is the most important out of these because you will also likely be posting YouTube videos on your other social media platforms. If you're editing and shooting a video, then your best bet will be to upload it to YouTube and then share it on Facebook or Twitter rather than using three separate video uploaders. This way, you can track who is seeing the video and how many people might be watching from beginning to end. When you have all of your analytics in one place, it will be easier to see where you are doing well and where you need to make more improvement.

Luckily, people have already done much of the work for you. Whatever your videos might be, there is likely some form of it online already. Though you might have a completely unique video idea that no one else has come close to creating, there still has to be something online that you can compare it to, whether it's a comedy skit, instructional video, or review. You should try to find the top videos that fall into the category in which you will be sharing your own content.

Look at all of those videos that already exist online. Look at the ones that have the most views, the most likes, and the pages with the most subscriptions. Go to your trending page and see what ones are sticking out the most. Look at the most viewed of all time, and also look at the most viewed within the past week, month, and year. It is your job to study these videos to see what they have that you can incorporate into your own marketing strategy.

Is there something about the way they are posting that makes their videos so desirable to watch? Is it the title of the video that's drawing viewers in, or are their videos successful because of the thumbnail? Look at the videos that are most relevant to your brand, and also make sure you are merely looking at the videos that draw your attention. Even if it's not related to the type of thing you're going to be posting, go to the home page and see which videos you make want to click them. When you can start to use your own taste and strategies and mix them with the ones that are already effective, then you will find the most successful way for you to post videos and grow your brand.

Before getting into the analytics and some information about to get more clicks, we need to remember what your videos are talking about at the core. Be sure that you have a strong message in your video that is clearly expressed to the viewers. Don't make your video confusing, and don't leave it with little to no point at all. Have a purpose for posting the video. Make sure that you are providing new content, and always have an apparent reason that someone would want to click on your video over the competitor's videos. Look at your competition to see what's missing and provide that to your viewers.

You have to get people talking about you. Even if it might be a bit controversial, having a discussion is going to be very helpful as well. You don't want to blatantly upset people just to get them speaking about you either. You have to make sure that you're still creating a video with meaning and not one only to troll and get likes. Don't be afraid to post something, however, because getting people talking can have them clicking on your video and giving you more views as well. You have to make sure that people are discussing the content that is being shared with others.

The more present and relevant you are on YouTube, the more you will be present on YouTube for other users. If you have 100,000 views on a video, that means it will be more likely to be seen than a video that only has 1,000 views. The more that you grow, the more potential you have to increase even further, and that's important to remember, especially when starting off. You might not hit it big or get it right the first time, but once you do, that will bring you the success that you've been waiting for.

Frequency

You should be posting at least three times a week to start off. As you go on, you might find that you will be posting less and less but give people the consistency and the content they want in the first place. This will also be your chance to try out new things and see what might work and what might need to be cut. You could try to do three different videos a week for three months. Then, at the end of the month, you might find that all kinds of videos have consistent viewers, but not every one of your followers watches all three videos. Then, you could decide to do one video a week for a month, and instead of picking which types out of the three original to continue, you combine all three. This could have the potential to triple your viewers, but you just have to make sure that you're starting off by posting more frequently.

It lets people know that they can rely on you for fresh content when you're posting more frequently. If you're only posting once a month or less, then people might not subscribe. There are some followers that are going to want to keep their subscriber number lower than the number of videos that they're consistently getting, so if you don't post often, they might not bother to subscribe. When you post more content as well, people will become reliant on your new videos. Then, when you don't have new content, and they're wanting more, they might go back to your old videos to re-watch or see if they can get their fix of your brand by visiting other social media pages and going to your website.

Remember not to be too spammy either. You don't want your content to clog up someone's news feed. While it's important to post consistently if you're doing three videos a day, then you're taking up space in everyone's feed, and they might not be as willing to continue to follow you. People want to rely on you for new content, but they also don't want to have only to see your posts over and over again.

Creating Playlists

This is a way to organize your videos for your viewers. You can create playlists based on different topics, shows, or other categories you choose on YouTube. This is an excellent way to "hack" the YouTube algorithm, as it helps you categorize your videos while lumping them in with others. Playlists show up on search feeds as well, so people might end up watching your entire playlist when they were really just searching for one video that would have been satisfied with a simple click had they not seen your playlist.

You're encouraging people to watch more of your videos. If people can see that you have a clear playlist made for them of songs, for example, then they will click and listen to that because it is more convenient than searching for ten different songs.

It categorizes them, so you know what the video is about more clearly. A video that might not have shown up in one search might still get watched by that person who did the searching because it was added to your playlist. This is also a way that you can make sure your followers are being provided with new content. If you create a playlist on a day that you don't post a video, it will still show in your follower's feed. They will then be reminded of your videos and watch, or they might watch out of curiosity because they are hoping that you did include a new video.

Descriptions and Titles

Use a headline analyzer tool to check the SEO score of your title. There are many different sites that you can go to where you can copy your exact title and paste it into their website. They will then tell you whether or not this is a good title for you to use based on what others are going to be posting. If you aren't familiar already, SEO is "search engine optimization," which basically means how likely your video will be to show up when someone searches a specific word or phrase. The higher your SEO score, the better chances your video will reach out to viewers that aren't even following you.

Do not use a clickbait headline if you are not going to provide that content. You could post "most amazing video you'll ever see" as a title to a rather mediocre advertisement, and you'll drive clicks. However, your watch time will be low, and that can damage your video and your analytics. People will also dislike the video, so luring someone in and not giving them what they want is only going to hurt you in the end. Watch time is driven by engagement, and that's going to help people keep up with your channel. When your watch time is higher, which means that more people that click on your video are sticking around to see it from start to finish, it will have a higher chance of showing up in other people's feeds and different searches they make relating to your video.

Your impressions are how many times your video will show up on a suggested page just merely by it being refreshed. Feelings increase with interactivity and views, so it's going to be important that your video is satisfying and engaging. If you post something that initially draws people in, only to eventually let them down, then you might get 100,000 views in a day, but then that'll be it. Your video won't have as many impressions on the pages of other videos being watched, and it's not going to show up in search engines, because YouTube's algorithm ensures that it's only going to provide people with quality content they want to see.

Tagging

Look at the tags that others are using. If you go to a YouTube video, you can find more information about it in a few ways. First, you can see the apparent words that are used in the video, such as what the author chose to name the video or what words exist in their description. After that, you can right-click on the video to find more about the source information, and you might get taken to a page filled with a bunch of codes. If you search the page by word and locate the keyword section, you can see exactly what the author used to tag their video. You could copy and paste these tags and use them in your own video, while also adding even more tags of your own! Do not be afraid to take advantage of all the tagging you can do to your video.

Vida is a great tool that helps you to see the analytics of specific tags that are being used. This way, you can see if your tags are going to be relevant, or if you should just delete them and make room for others. Just make sure that you aren't using any tags not relevant to you. The tag "cake decorating" might be the most searched of the week, but if your video is on how to change a tire, that's completely unrelated. If that shows up in the search for someone doing a cake decorating, they are only going to get frustrated and dislike your video. It will also be a way that you're targeting an audience that isn't even relevant to your brand. If you have the means to do so, you should caption your videos as well. This way, you are adding even more tags, because YouTube's algorithm uses the captions of videos to help determine what videos will show up in different searches. If someone searches for a video using words that are in your captions, then your video will have a higher chance of showing up. We also need to consider those viewers that can't hear or won't be watching YouTube with the volume up when making our videos. These people will appreciate that your videos are captioned, and you have yet again tapped into a substantial audience.

Style and Design

You could hack the YouTube algorithm, but if you don't show a unique brand and style, then it's not going to get you as far as the profiles that stand out more. One good thing to remember is how color can play an essential part in your videos. You want to make sure that you are including at least one color and that your videos aren't all just black and white. A color that works really well for people is red, as it makes them feel alert. If you use a red arrow or a red circle in your thumbnail, it brings your viewers eyes there thinking that they should click and watch.

Look at the thumbnails of the top videos that are cycling around "trending" and "most viewed." Look at what images and colors they're using, and see which ones draw your eyes towards it the most. This will give you an idea of what you should be incorporating in your video. Just because something doesn't catch your eye, that doesn't mean other people don't see the appeal.

Clean Up Old Videos

You might be affecting the views of your next video if the last one didn't do that well. YouTube will sometimes simply play the next video that was uploaded after a certain one depending on that user's algorithm. If your next video didn't do so well, it would have less of a chance in showing up. For example, let's say video #1 has 10,000 views, video #2 has 345, and video #3 has 3,400. If someone clicks on video #1 and watches it through, there's a good chance that YouTube's algorithm is going to see that not many people watched video #2, and instead direct the viewer to another person's page. If you delete video #2, then YouTube's algorithm will see that video #3 is more successful and has a higher rate of growth, so they will direct viewers to your next video, keeping that user on your page.

Target People That Want to See Your Videos

Your video could reach 200,000 people, but if your video is about reviewing iPhones and you only hit 1,000 tech viewers and 190,000 beauty vlog viewers, then you're not doing that well for your channel overall. This is why proper tagging is so important. If you are too broad, then you're going to have trouble finding your niche. Instead, make sure you are starting small with the audience that will care about your content more. Then, you can grow it and take it to a place where more people will like and see your video.

The Actual Video

First, you have to figure out if you're going to be using your channel for brand awareness or simply to get views and collect ad revenue. Both of these are excellent options but picking out one can help you decide what videos to use and what audience you should try and target.

Ideally, your videos will show both, but at first, you might need to try new things to really establish your brand. Videos that are for brand awareness are good because you can make them sponsored videos. You have to pay for this feature, but this means that your content will show up as an official advertisement before and within specific videos. You can also post these videos on different social media accounts and get even more views. If you're creating your video to inform or get attention, this is also good because it will help you get opinions, and it's a form of brand awareness in and of itself.

First and foremost, you'll want your video to show off who you are but remember that YouTube might have different users then who your followers are on your other platforms. Look at the analytics of your followers on other social media platforms so you can understand if you're going to be finding the same type of people on YouTube as well.

Length

The longer your videos are, the higher the chance that you will get more ad revenue. Make sure that you aren't only using this as a way to make money, however. You also want your content to be shareable and watchable. If all your videos are 30 minutes, then it's less likely that people are going to share those videos on their own social media. Having long videos is still essential depending on your content, but make sure that you are offering shorter videos as well.

Having shortened versions of your videos will be very important. These shorter versions could be things that you decide to share on your other social media platforms. You could give a 10-second teaser on your Instagram for a 10-minute video on YouTube. You could also provide a 3-minute breakdown of a 45-minute video on Facebook. Whatever you choose, make sure you are giving your viewers more than one kind of video.

Chapter 5:
How to Use Instagram for Further Exposure

Instagram started as just a way that you could post more beautiful and inspiring pictures. It came after Facebook, which was already inclusive of people posting images. Only, the images on Instagram were different. They were of higher quality, and you aren't expected to post as many. Instagram offered filters for its photographs, and people would only be given the option to post square images. This was different because it became not only important to make sure that your individual post looked good, but that your entire Instagram aesthetic matches as well.

Instagram not only plays a significant role in millions of people's lives but for some individuals, it has become their sole form of income. There are individual big Instagram names that can make a few hundred thousand dollars a post, and many people following in their footsteps that are hoping to find the same amount of fame. People are even creating accounts for their pets, and making money from those accounts, doing sponsorships with different pet treat and clothing brands! There are hundreds of millions of users on Instagram, and each and every one of those people can be a potential customer to your brand or product. They don't even have to follow you, and there's still a chance that they can be exposed to what it is that you are choosing to sell.

Instagram has changed the way that other social media sites look at their marketing tactics altogether. There is more of a focus on advertising in a way that is personal to viewers. Organic marketing is just as important as paid advertisements, and social media sites are aware of this. In fact, that is what has changed a lot of the algorithms, such as Facebook and YouTube, to show users content that is meaningful over things that are advertorial.

As an established brand, you can find benefits from posting in two different ways. On the one hand, you can simply post to grow your following, and from there, you can advertise yourself and your products so that people buy directly from you. Instagram is also great because it can help so many different collaborators get together and work towards a common goal, where they find mutual benefits that keep their following and customer count growing.

Why Instagram Is Important

Instagram doesn't quite have a billion users yet, but it's clear that the numbers are going to be getting there faster than we can realize. It's a bit newer than Facebook or YouTube, so just because it's not there yet doesn't mean that it won't be. At first, people avoided Instagram because it was more limiting than other social media. It has managed to find new ways of innovation and methods that users can create individual posts while still maintaining a lot of things that brought users there in the first place.

People respond the best to ads that seem natural, not something that is forced upon them. Instagram is a new way that innovators can do this. Many celebrities will post pictures of themselves, stating how much they like the brand and how you should buy it as well. It used to take thousands of dollars to get celebrities to do this. They would often have to go and shoot an entire commercial, and when we would watch it on TV, we would mute or walk away, not paying attention because we knew it was an ad.

Now, many people will wake up in the morning, take a lunch break, or simply sit on the couch and check in on their social media. They voluntarily follow certain celebrities, and these people will share ads with their followers. People are going to pay attention to this more than a paid advertisement they see in their feed because they trust that person. They followed them for a reason and are buying into their brand. Therefore, they're going to be a lot more likely to buy into their products.

Instagram is a new way that we can market our brands, and we have to establish ourselves now. The more we can integrate ourselves into people's news feeds, the longer we will be around for the growing years that lie ahead. Though Instagram is going to be around for a long time to come, we still have to make sure that we're getting on the platform now.

On a simple level, you want to get on before your username gets taken! On a deeper level, you'll want to establish your brand now and get in with people before they are too overwhelmed with all the companies they have to face on their feed. As Instagram grows, so does the competition, which means so do the options for the customers that you're going to want to target.

Posting Strategies

You have to be very meticulous with how you choose to post on Instagram. Instagram used to simply show users what pictures were published in a particular chronological order. Now, they use an algorithm similar to Facebook in that they aim to show their users only meaningful content. This means that if you're posting too much, too little, or the wrong things, you might not end up in someone's feed even though they're following you.

Instagram isn't just dependent on what comes up first. Instead, its curates' users' feeds so that they are shown the things they seem to want to see the most. This will be based on the other people they follow, what other people like, and the things that they love themselves. How often they visit a page will affect that, and their likelihood to comment or leave a heart will also change the chances of a post showing up in their feed. All of this simply means that you have to post only pictures that your followers want to see. Instagram is different than other sites because you have to be very clean and specific with your content.

An excellent posting strategy is to post no more than once a day. You might think you have a higher chance of being in someone's feed if you post more, but if you do this, you are just putting a higher chance on your things going unseen by different users.

Finding Optimal Results

Instagram is owned by Facebook, so you will see optimal results when you can incorporate the two. You can share what you post on Instagram straight to Facebook, so this is a perfect way to make sure that your posts are being seen by both followers. You can share your Instagram on your Facebook as well so that people know they should check you out on both places.

You also have to ensure that you are transforming your material and growing your brand, not staying stagnant with one kind of design. While it can be easy to find a "theme" and stick to that, make sure you aren't being too specific. Having a brand isn't just about only posting one kind of picture, or images that include a particular color. You have to give off an overall aesthetic and appeal so that when someone sees your picture, they know it's you before you even reveal that it is an image that belongs to your company.

Your brand has to be one that people want to follow. This is why individuality is so important. If your brand is similar to someone else's, then why would someone that already follows that first brand chooses to follow you? Give people a reason to choose you. Provide them with something that they need, something that they've been missing. People will create their identity with their social media, and your company should be one that people want to be a part of.

Establishing Images

Your images are going to be very important when creating your marketing strategies. You want to make sure that you are posting things that are readily identifiable as belonging to you. The first thing people are going to look at is your picture. They will then read your caption and see that it's your account, but first they will be judging the image. Make sure that it's something that clearly shows off who you are. At the same time, don't stick so tightly to your "theme" that it shows up as another generic post on someone's feed. Always find new and innovative ways to share your brand.

When people like your brand, they're more often than not going to like your pictures even if they don't entirely like the message. For example, if you're a clothing brand and you post an image of someone in a dress, you will get people to like that picture if it's a beautiful image. Some of those people will go onto buying the dress, and the rest won't. Out of the people that don't, some might not have the money to. Others might not obtain the suit because they would never wear it themselves. They still liked the picture, however, and all their followers will be able to see that they wanted your image as well. This helps make sure that your posts are being exposed to other users.

Make sure your images are clear and easy to read. If you post a closeup of something hard to decipher or an image that's been reposted to the point that it's pixelated, people aren't going to be as interested in your vision. Make it as professional as possible and have a comment that is meticulously curated as well.

Your images should also provide information to different users. If someone comes across your picture that doesn't follow you, then you will want to make sure you've successfully conveyed your message in a clear way so that they can see who you are before they even choose to follow you.

Creating Your Brand

An excellent way to build your brand and stick to it is by selecting different filters that will match each other. You could pick out a filter that adds a tan tone to everything, and when people click on your page, all your pictures will match because you decided to make them all the same sound. This is a great way to keep people interested in your page and aware of your brand.

Don't look at your own post. Look at how your position interacts with other peoples on an explore type page. Whenever you are about to take a picture, go to your own explore page. Look at the photos that you want to click on the most. Does the image that you are going to post have the same "clickable" factors that the most liked photos on your explore page do?

Imagine how your post is going to fit in with the rest of your page. If something randomly sticks out, then it might break things up and make you look sloppy, giving people the idea that you don't have a strong brand. If your company's identity is weak, then it's not going to be something that others are as willing to associate themselves with. Use Instagram stories for pictures that might not always fit in with your aesthetic.

Now that you know the importance of putting your brand out there and reaching new followers let's look at some of the algorithmic secrets behind Instagram.

Chapter 6:
Reverse Engineering Instagram

The way that Instagram works is that it shows you photos based on your interest, timeliness, and relationship. It used to simply show users things based on the order that they were posted. This caused a lot of people to miss out on older posts and would also give them the things that they might not have been in interested as seeing. Instagram's mission is to get people to use their app as often as possible, so they are going to do what it takes to make the users happy first, and then those that want to advertise. To do this successfully, they have to cater a news feed to what someone wants to see and not just what's going to make everyone the most money.

Interest determines if you will like a picture or if you will simply keep scrolling. Your investment isn't just what you're going to want to see the most, but also what you're going to like the most. This might be why you see your friends' pictures more than the celebrities you follow. There's a better chance that you and your sibling are liking each other's photos more than you and the most developed models on Instagram are sharing likes with each other.

Timelines deal with how recently you posted that photo, or when a photo was posted. So, while a picture from two weeks ago might have more likes than a picture posted yesterday, Instagram still takes time into consideration when choosing to show you an image based on their algorithm.

Your relationship is going to deal with how you know a specific person that makes a post. Again, this will include how many times you and another person are sharing likes. This differs just from interest in that it also considers how often you might tag them, be tagged by them, chat in the comments, and chat in messenger. The more you do this, and the more you have an online relationship with someone, the more their posts are going to show up in your feed.

Now, this means that you can use all of those things to your advantage. When creating your Instagram marketing strategy, remember these three things that Instagram relies on for their algorithm. Interest, timeliness, and relationship are going to be the most important things determining if your post is going to end up in the feed of your followers.

While we can understand how the Instagram algorithm works, there are also some other factors that we need to consider. First and foremost, some people on Instagram will follow a ton of people at once. There is no limit to how many people you can follow, so some individuals who are subscribed to your account might also be following 3,000 other pages.

Frequently, these people won't even be actively looking at their feed and instead just look people up correctly when they are searching for other individuals. In addition to this, we also have to factor in that what they want to see the most is going to pop up based on what they like.

A person isn't going to look at 3000 different pictures a day, and if they do, then that's a rarity because most of us do have other things to do - like work full-time work or study in school. It is going to be our job, then, as an influencer, to make sure that we are reaching as many of our followers as possible while also ensuring that the ones already following us can see, like, and comment even though they might have hundreds of people already competing for their attention.

Some users might only get on once a week, or they might barely spend time on the app at all. Though a person has an account, that doesn't guarantee that they are going to be using their mind as much as the rest of your followers. So, people will either fall somewhere in between having a ton of followers, and your content gets lost in their feed, or people rarely get on at all.

These are going to be the two extremes, and you're going to want to try and find a way to hit that demographic that's in between. A lot of people on the app will only be following a couple hundred people, and they will get on relatively regularly, so it's not like we have to panic. There are just some ways that will work better for a brand, depending on your followers and other techniques that might not work at all. It's up to us to decide.

Luckily, there is no difference between how much your business profile and personal profile might reach followers through organic reach. On Facebook, there is going to be more of a limitation on what your followers can see based on whether your profile is personal or a business one. When it comes to Instagram, this is not going to be the case. You have just as much of a chance of reaching a follow with organic reach as a business profile as you would a personal account. People are still going to be more likely to see the things that they have a higher chance of liking, but at the same time, they won't be filtered from your business profile.

Another way that you can increase your chances of reaching out to followers is to encourage them to tag you in their own posts. If someone shares your account on their own, then you are getting free advertisement by them exposing you to all of their followers. This could mean reaching thousands of more people depending on who follows them. And if you can get a celebrity to tag you, well, that's even better! There are many reasons why someone would want to tag you in their post. Firstly, to encourage users to share you in their content that might be related to yours. For example, let's pretend that you have a business Instagram account for your dog product brand. You might encourage your followers to tag you in their cutest dog pictures. This would be a great way to reach out to your followers and figure out who is already interacting consistently with your content.

Alternatively, you can encourage your followers to tag you with their products that have been purchased. If you're a furniture company, then it would be a great idea to help your followers to tag you in their pictures, including them using your items. This is an excellent method for marketing because the followers of those people that tag you will be more likely to trust you with their products because they see that a person, they loyally follow use your items, knowing that they will likely have the same experience should they choose you.

Post things that tell them to tag a friend as well. Not as many people will be willing to post a picture on their feed just to show off your product, and they might follow you but still not have made a purchase, so this kind of encouragement won't work for every type of Instagram account. Especially if you're a personal account, then telling followers to tag their friends and followers in your post gives them the chance to bring people to your page with little to no effort from you.

Whatever your content is, it should be relatable so that you can be sure your followers will want to share it with the people that they connect the most with online. Maybe you post a funny meme or image and say, "tag a friend that can relate." You could even simply post a funny picture and say, "tag a friend that looks like this." Another one that is often seen is an account with a product that will tell their followers, "tag someone that needs this" or something along those lines. You've given them a prompt, a call to action, so they are more likely to participate in that post and generate the engagement that you need to keep consistent traffic coming back to your page.

Now, it's time to really look at the psychology of what you're posting to get people to interact with your content. The thing about the human brain is that it can cause us to do things without us even consciously realizing it even when we are awake. Though we like to think we are in total control of the content we consume and the things we want to look at and share with other friends, there is a lot about our psychology that is out of our control.

It might seem like you just like something just because, or for seemingly no reason, but there is always a reason. There will always be underlying psychological factors that can help drive decisions, even if you can't think of them yourself. It's up to you, then, as a marketer and someone that's selling their brand online, to make sure that you are aware of these factors so that you can include them into your own content marketing strategy.

Customers are more likely to follow pages with clear images than posts that have a lot of text. For every 10 posts of pictures that people see, they will remember the photos of 8 of those posts. When it comes to images with text, they will only remember 2 out of 10.

This shows that you need to put an emphasis on actual images and pictures, not just creating text. The most powerful images that you should try to incorporate with your brand will be those that can tell the story and do all the talking without you having to provide a large amount of explanatory text. People also like to have choices - but not too many. When you're trying to get them to engage and even when you're making a sale on a particular product, make sure that you are giving them more than one option, but fewer than 5 or 6 to choose from so that they aren't feeling overwhelmed.

Make sure that you are picking an overall aesthetic. People like consistency, so it's up to you to decide what content you're going to be sharing regularly. Your aesthetic will be a combination of the types of images you show, the material inside these images, the coloring of your choice, and the overall feeling and emotions that the model gives off when people are looking at it.

If you are showing off your brand, you are also letting people know that you care about what it is that you have created, not just that you're trying to get people to sell something. Having a brand and aesthetically show that you are creative, innovative, and passionate. If all of your images are just there as separate pieces and don't really have anything that connects them, then your pictures aren't going to last in people's minds. They won't be as ingrained as quickly.

Don't create content that is off-topic. Once you determine what your theme is, you have to stick to it. When it comes to picking a color, you have to be aware of the types of colors that can represent different feelings and moods. Let's start with red. Red is an alert. It lets people know that their attention is required by you and that you are trying to share with them something that they need to pay attention to. The biggest brands that use red as their color will likely be the top of their market, outcompeting other brands that might choose a different color.

Orange is going to be a little friendlier and might be used for brands that are "for all." Yellow is a little warmer, letting people know that their brand is optimistic and something they can trust. Alternatively, yellow can also provide the kind of clarity that's important for many followers when choosing a reliable brand. Green is more associated with the environment and health.

Anytime you see a brand that has green, you can assume it has something to do with nature, plants, animals, and health. Blue shows trust and dependency. The type of blue (aqua/teal) doesn't make much of a difference, though a dark versus light blue might indicate the kind of strength that the brand is trying to give off. Blue is among the most popular color for the top brands because people want to subscribe to a brand that provides them with the trust needed for the top companies. Purple will be most often associated with any kind of creative product. If something is a little more innovative while also including a sort of artistic aesthetic, then blue is going to work well. Pink is for feminine brands and will be associated with things that are made for women. Aside from that, pink can be used for children and just anything that wants to give off the feeling of being soft and innocent.

Black can be associated often with anything more glamorous, luxurious, and overall trying to give off a feeling of wealth. It will be sleek and expensive, or at least that will be the aesthetic that the brand choosing black might be trying to give off. If a brand decides to use white for their aesthetic, then they are showing they are cool, calm, and clean. This is another popular color because it is more blank than the others, allowing wiggle room for the marketing strategies that they might decide to use.

Find a way to relate to someone's emotions. This isn't just a sad emotion, either. Our feelings are based on the beliefs that we already have and the things that we've experienced. There are a lot of emotions that will make people relate to one another, but at the end of the day, our feelings are still based on our personal identities, which are unique to anyone else.

Some things that are clearly sad, such as an abandoned puppy, will relate to a lot of people and can really tug on their heartstrings. However, those who have dogs of their own versus those who dislike dogs altogether are going to have very different levels of emotion that will keep them interested in whatever the subject might be relating to the abandoned puppy. We have to keep in mind the profound emotional impact that many of our viewers and followers have the potential to elicit when consuming our content.

When you can grab onto a person's emotions, they will be more likely to interact, and drive interest toward your content. As much as we might like to think that we are creatures based on reason and logic, our emotions will really be what seals the deal at the end of the day. If you're trying to choose between two homes when you're house shopping, you're going to look at the logistics first. One house is closer to work, but one house has lower monthly payments.

We can outweigh the benefits and positives of our decisions based on reason, but our emotions will help us create the conclusions needed to make that final choice. You will look at the benefits that each of the two houses has, but the one that you can envision your family in, the one with a nostalgic factor, or one that is closer to your family is going to be the one that you pick because this is what your emotions told you.

We have to remember this the most when it comes to marketing. Like we said earlier, emotions are more than just feeling sad. These are happy feelings, angry thoughts, frustrated moods, grumpy days, and everything else that drives the way that we hold onto and express our emotions overall. Make your customers laugh, give them something that feels good, remind them of the injustices that make them angry.

Whatever it is, you have to start using their own emotions to help not only drive a sale but to keep them as loyal followers that will continue to come back to you over and over again.

Give your followers a "call to action." This is going to be anything that encourages them to interact. When you can make them feel as though they need to take action to do something, then you will make a sale more easily on whatever it is that you're encouraging them to buy. One of the best calls to actions that can lead to a deal is to make your followers feel like there is a sense of urgency. Tell them that a particular product is going really fast or that they need to make a purchase now because they will miss out on the sale. If you do this, then they will feel more pressured to make a decision, and those that were on the edge of whether or not they wanted to buy will know that now is their chance.

Even people that might not have been initially interested will follow through and at least see if there is something they can get for a good deal because they don't want to miss out. Giving this urgency also creates a sort of group that your followers will want to become a part of. If you say, "now is your last chance to get our newest product! They won't last much longer! Only a few left!" or any variation of this, you are automatically letting your followers know that this product is very exclusive and in high demand. When others think that they need to take advantage of this high demand, then they will be more likely to follow through with a sale because they want to be "in" on that trend.

If you want to create a group urgency for your friends as well, make sure that you are using ""you" r" sentences and phrasing. Don't say, "link in bio for exclusive deals."

Say, "link in bio to see *your* exclusive deals." This alone gives them more of an independent feeling and makes your followers think that they are more exclusive than others because they have content catered to them. Another call to action method is to simply get them actually to take action. Tell them to go outside and get moving while using your product. Tell them that they should travel and receive your product with them.

Depending on what it is that you're selling with your brand, you can find an actual action that exists outside of the Internet world that you can encourage your followers to do. Even if it's not related explicitly to your brand, encouraging them to go out and do something will help make sure your images are sticking in their head. Even posting something like, "do one thing that makes you happy today," will be associated with you and your brand.

You can be a lotion company, and a follower sees that post, then decides to watch a movie later that night. Even though the two things aren't related, your follower might still think of you when they are doing that thing that makes them happy, helping to increase your brand awareness. The more you can associate your brand with your followers' lives outside of the online world, the easier it will be to actually create a loyal following.

Make sure that you are posting regularly. This means doing it a few times a day or maybe even every other day, but definitely somewhere in between that amount. Depending on your content, you don't want to overload your followers. A fashion brand should post more frequently than one that provides a more specific service. If your brand is more readily associated with images, as a personal brand would be, then you would post more than something that falls into a niche. Make sure that your posts are spread throughout. The best time to post is when people are likely going to be on their phones.

This will include the morning, right when people are waking up and when they're getting ready for work. The next time that would be good to post is when people are on their lunch breaks or at least the middle of the day when they might be getting bored and want to wander onto the web. After people are getting off of school and work, between 3-5 pm, is a great time as well. If people hadn't been able to check their phone during their lunch breaks, then they're certainly going to make sure that they are doing so now.

Then, posting after dinner is going to be a good time as well, maybe between 8-10 pm. After that, you might want to hold off on posting. Though people are going to be scrolling on their phone late at night while watching TV or lying in bed, you don't want always to post because they might have other content to get caught up on, and yours can get lost in the rest. If your brand is more of a late-night one, maybe for adult products, alcohol, or something else that would hit the audience that stays up late, then, by all means, don't wait until 8 am to post. Of course, you want to cater when you post to your target audience, but these are just the times that most people are likely to be online.

Don't post a ton at once either. Posting consistently means spreading out your images. Though you might be someone busy that don't have time to post all day online, you still want to spread out the posts, or else your followers will feel like you're trying to spam their feed. If you struggle to post throughout, you have the option to save some as drafts so that you don't have to worry about the post taking too long. Whatever your call to action is, make it as simple as possible. Don't overexplain yourself and find ways to shorten sentences to make them seem like more straightforward tasks.

Don't just wait for people to interact on your own page as well. You might decide to reach out to some other people and comment on their posts to see if that could draw attention towards your page. You could also try and tap into some of your followers' pages, maybe thanking them that they bought your product or tagged you, or you could tell them that they look great while wearing your products. Don't reach out to every follower though or you'll spend a lot of time doing so.

This is something brands will try to do. It can work for some, but it could also make you look spammy and desperate. Try to limit who you're commenting towards at first. Choose people with Instagram's that have a lot of followers, people that post consistently, and followers that seem to have a particular brand and aesthetic.

Your Instagram bio is going to be just as important as everything else that you post. A lot of companies will overlook the bios they create and instead simply focus on the texts that they include in their posts more than anything. Your bio can consist of hashtags that could help draw people to your page. It is also a great place to store all your links that might help followers get driven to your other websites and pages. You have the option of saving your stories as well so that your followers will be more likely to review old highlights of the story that you had on your profile. You can also include a section where people can send you emails directly so that you are very easy to reach out to.

If you try to always post a ton of information in your picture and post descriptions, then it's going to be really confusing for your followers, and they're going to have trouble keeping interested. Your bio can be where you clearly layout info for followers so that they don't have to go hunting for the vital information.

Find collaborations that will "pay" in followers rather than actual money. Sometimes we don't always have it in the budget to pay for a partnership with someone else, and that can be damaging to our brand. Look for a way that you can trade things with other accounts similar to you and simultaneously have benefits to your business.

For example, let's say that you're a clothing store in a medium-sized city, and you want to gain followers. You could find a brand similar to yours, for example, a restaurant in the same town, and team up. Both of you might have about 5,000 followers, and the two of you could use more to keep businesses consistent and traffic to your page more frequent. One way to do this would be to have a contest or special giveaway that the two of you are in charge of.

You can both come up with the regulations for how to enter, but one of the rules is that all participants must be following both of you. This will cause the other brand's followers to go to your page while your followers go to their page, potentially doubling your followers, if everyone participated in the contest, that is. The giveaway can be a gift card to your store or even just a discount.

By doing this, you reach out to a new audience and one that is close to your brand, meaning that the followers are more likely to stick around after the contest. It will have cost you almost nothing, other than the discount for your brand, but that will still create a customer that is more likely to come back.

Another fun way to drive user interaction is to let people "take over" your account. This is something that you would want to do if you have more followers and a budget to pay an influencer. How this would work is you would find a personal brand with a lot of active followers that match your style.

You can ask them to take over your account for a day, where they would post exclusive content, maybe go live, or do a Q & A. whatever they want to do is up to them. When they are taking over, then they have the chance to bring the followers they have to your page, potentially increasing followers. This is also just a fun way to do things and gets people excited about both brands.

Don't be afraid to use marketing towards your Instagram in the offline marketing world. We get so focused on making sure everything stays online and relevant to social media that we forget there's an entire market of users not online as well. Create posters in your businesses that encourage followers. You can even offer a discount to people in-store only if they show proof that they are already following you. This will help connect the real world to the online world, making your account much more likely to attract new followers.

Tell A Story with Your Posts

Your posts need to inform your users. They want to feel a personal connection with you. This is how Instagram differs from any other form of social media. It is a lot more private. They are choosing to "follow" you when there's a good chance that they won't get a follow back. There has to be a purpose to this, and you have to provide them with the content that they want to see. If you're just posting annoying updates or the same things that can be seen elsewhere, then there is no longer a purpose for your followers to choose to stay subscribed to you.

As a small business owner, don't be afraid to brand yourself as a person and not just as your company. Keeping separate accounts can be essential but tag yourself and your employees in pictures so followers can connect with the people behind the posts. If you share personal updates and allow yourself, or another person, to become the face of your product or service, then you are giving people a more intimate look into the things that they are spending their money on.

Make sure that you are using your story just as often as you're making individual posts as well. You should really be posting more on your accounts, making sure you do at least two or three times a day. People might scroll through their feed within twenty minutes, and it could take all day for new posts to emerge. What they'll do in the meantime, then, is check their explore page and their stories. Stories are essential for making sure your followers remember and care about your brand while also informing them of deals or sales they could take advantage of that are coming from your brand.

Tagging

Tagging is going to be everything when you're first starting off. This is going to be the way that you connect users that have no idea who you are to your content. It is a way to grow followers while also ensuring that you're providing information to your current followers. To get a good sense of tagging, rather than looking at a picture, first, look at that specific tag. The images that have the most likes are the ones that are the most relevant, so this is important to remember. Just like on YouTube, you wouldn't use a tag that has no relevance over your post or else you are just going to make people look past your brand. You'll also be targeting the wrong audiences, so you're getting exposure, but not a high amount of people that will follow and buy into your brand.

Location tags open you up to others around you that are interested in your kinds of posts. You never want to put your exact location down, such as your personal address just to protect yourself. However, tag in public settings all you want and use a general city tag to make people aware of your travels. By doing this, you're connecting your posts with other people's posts that are occurring in the same area. For example, someone might post a picture of their birthday party and tag their location of Los Angeles. Then, if they're bored, they might go through that tag and look at other pictures, seeing your delicious plate of food that you tagged at your own restaurant. That person might like or follow you based on the post, or, even better, they might go to your restaurant. By using this tag, you're connecting to others and exposing your page.

People tagging is going to be crucial in making sure that your brand is reaching more than just the apparent upfront users. When someone comes to your restaurant and is taking pictures, ask if you can use their image and tag them! Then, when people that follow them look at their tagged photos, they'll see that they were at your restaurant and that's another person that you've exposed your brand to. You don't want to be pushy with how you approach people, and instead, you could encourage them to post and tag with different signs or notable novelties at your location. Still, tagging people will help boost Instagram's algorithm in your favor.

Hash tagging is a big part of Instagram that can get many users exposed to new pictures, places, and things as well. The beauty is that you can use as many hashtags as you want. Remember relevance with regular hash tagging too and do it in your picture's caption rather than the comments, as this is more likely to get it to end up on the top page for that particular hashtag.

Making Sure Your Content Is Shareable

Sharing is how many people will interact with their friends on Instagram. They can share your posts through messages, or they can tag their friends in the comments on your post. Give users something that they really want to show their friends. With an Instagram business profile, you can start to see just how many people might be sharing your content.

By using what we discussed in this section, you could grow your followers to as much as 10,000 directly with organic marketing, tagging, and creating shareable content. In the rest of the chapter, we're going to show you how you can make that number even higher.

Reaching Out to Followers

Instagram's algorithm includes showing users posts based on how often they use the app and how many people they are following. If there is a user that is on Instagram for three hours a day, and they're following 500 people, they are likely going to see all of their posts from who they follow. If someone follows 500 people and only gets on for an hour every three days, they are going to see just the very top of the posts that they've missed. When you're choosing who to follow, you must go for people that are following fewer people. You should also look at their activity and see if they post frequently or not because this can determine how often they're getting online.

Always thank your customers when they share that they supported your business. This should go without saying and is something we mentioned previously, but it is very crucial you do on Instagram. People will likely tag your business in posts relating to your products, so it will be your chance to give them a thank you. It lets that customer know you care, the rest of your followers that you care, and makes other people see that you're a brand that is concerned about their customers as well.

Follow your follower's followers. It sounds confusing, but it makes total sense. When you are looking for more people to follow, first go to your followers. See the people that they are following and choose to support them. This way, when that new person checks your page to see who you are, they will see that their friend is already following them. This then gives them the idea that you are more of a trustworthy brand that is worth they follow back.

Stories

Stories are a great way that you can post more content without having to worry about spamming your followers. People can easily skip through stories, and even without a business profile, you can easily track this information. This is important because it's what's going to help you determine if what you're posting is good or bad and if you should keep up with it or move onto something that might bring more success.

You can post when you put a new story on there as well so that way you can make sure your followers are looking at your posts. This will ensure that viewers will see your actual Instagram post even if it gets lost in their feed because of the algorithm. The next time that you choose to post something brand new to your Instagram page, make sure that you put a notification on your story, letting your followers know that you have uploaded new content.

Make your advertisements fit in with other people's stories as well. People don't want to be intruded on when they are watching their friend's stories with an ad that is too loud, too obnoxious, or too obvious. Instead, create advertisements that seem natural, as if they were personal stories themselves.

Saved stories is a great way that people can get more content from your account. When you have posted a story, before it expires, you can actually save that to your profile along with other older stories, even categorizing them, so people have an accessible way to click through your images.

Paid Advertisements

You can pay to have your posts appear on other people's feeds, or you could pay to have your ads as Instagram stories. Either way, remember that the same rules for paid advertisements pretty much go for regular posts. The only thing you have to be sure of with both is that you are not tricking people. Some laws protect users from getting deceived, and you have to make sure that you are letting people know if something is an #ad if you are doing a sponsorship with an individual company.

Your paid content is going to take some trial and error periods as well. Make sure that you do not pay for any marketing until you've done some organic marketing first. If you go into paid marketing blindly, then you might not find as much success and could end up losing money. Instead, be assured that you are only paying for things that you know will do the best so that you don't have to worry about losing any money.

Before you start with paid advertisements, you'll want to establish yourself for a couple of weeks at least first. This is plenty of time to try more than one method of marketing so that you are only putting money towards surefire ways to get your brand attention.

Instagram Mistakes

It's essential to know the mistakes you could make with the Instagram algorithm. Just like how other accounts have already done some of the dirty work to let us know what will help us find success, they've also gone through the more challenging parts, letting us know basic common mistakes and what not to do when using Instagram marketing.

There are some things you might want to do that seem like they'll obviously help you get more viewers. For one thing, following a thousand people might make you think that you'll get a thousand followers back. It isn't always this easy, however, so you have to have more specific strategies before going in.

The less you avoid the following sections, the more likely you'll be doing things that actually help you to get new followers.

Posting Right in A Row

You might think that posting five things right in a row is a surefire way to get people to see at least one of your posts. You should avoid doing this as much as possible, however. If you do this, your posts might be not ordered and confusing for your followers. Some people will make chronological posts in parts, but because of Instagram's algorithm, these videos will usually get broken up. Instead, make sure that you are clearly labeling things and that no one has to go searching through other images to get the things that they want.

Posting right in a row will make you seem more spammy as well. People won't mind seeing pictures every couple of days, but if they have to see your photos more than what their friends are posting, they're going to be more likely to unfollow.

Spamming Others

Make sure that you aren't spamming your new followers yet either. Some individuals will think that they will do well if they tag people or comment on all their stuff. You might have noticed from personal social media use that there are some individuals who will just blindly follow whoever. You go to their page and see that they have 20,000 followers, so they seem legitimate. Then, however, you notice that they're also following 4,000 people, so you can assume that they got most of those followers from doing a follow/unfollow tactic. Those work at first, but there are better ways that you can grow your following.

You don't want to bother people too much. They don't want to feel invaded. If you are too spammy, pushy, or present on someone's social media, they could end up getting annoyed to the point where they block you. Then, you will have lost them as a potential customer, and your things won't have much of a chance in showing up in their follower's explore pages either.

Being Too Business-Oriented

The point of social media was to make sure that you can connect closely with others. Instagram's that are too rigid or professional will find that they aren't as successful as brands that have a more personal touch. If all your posts are strictly about the company and only ever resembling ads that are selling people things, then you won't have as many followers. You might have sales, but you won't have people that will stick around and follow you, giving you more consistent business rather than a one-time deal.

Don't make your Instagram feel like a business. You'll undoubtedly want to support your brand and share your products, but if they feel like they are getting too spammed with your business, they're going to unfollow. We already have to deal with many different paid advertisements when we get on social media. If the non-sponsored posts and just the organic press that we see also feels like an ad, we're not going to like that brand and the chance of getting on the app as often have decreased as well.

If you look at some of the biggest companies, they don't always have that many followers. They're more likely to have a higher number of likes on Facebook. This is because people are choosing to hit "follow" for a specific reason. Give people an idea to follow you, not just a reason to "like" you.

Not Giving Enough Information

Don't lure your customers to your page by not providing enough information. Most of the time, they'll just look to the comments, so they don't have to leave the page altogether. People don't want to have to leave Instagram, because that's not the reason they were there in the first place. You might want to get them to go to your website, so they start spending money on products and services, but you should never trick them into doing so.

Make sure that you also let your followers, and those that are seeing your posts, know about your company rather than forcing them to follow you on social media. You might not want to give all the information away and leave some things for your followers, but you still want to make sure that people that don't know you can find out as much information as possible from a single post, description, or biography.

Chapter 7:
The Next Platform Facebook

Over 20 billion ad clicks come from Facebook each and every year. That's a lot of revenue that Facebook gets, as well as being a large amount of money towards the companies on the other end of the click as well.

Just because one ad click doesn't contribute to a sale, that doesn't mean it didn't still help drive brand awareness either. Sometimes, you might find that a click will be just that, but it could also be someone reminding themselves to go back to your page later. For example, they might stumble upon your page while at work. They can't look at your products for too long, so they leave your site. Later, when they're at home watching TV, they might end up going back to your site to do some shopping that they couldn't get away with at work.

Half of the traffic that goes to a website that uses Facebook marketing comes from Facebook! That's a huge factor and alone a critical thing to remember when you're deciding if you should be on Facebook in the first place. You could be missing out on a lot of website traffic. The thing is, when people leave Facebook to actually go to your website, they might even be more likely to buy your products than the customers that come to your page, not through social media.

Facebook also owns Instagram, so knowing that the two are at the top is an important thing to remember. Together, these make up one super tool that can drive your business from small to international. All you have to do is make sure that you are aware of the tools that both offer, and how to use them to your company's best abilities. If you're not on either of these platforms, you're doing a big disservice to your business.

What You Want to Promote

Facebook has a lot of different content, so it's going to be very important that you pick out what you want to market before deciding how to trade. It seems to be obvious, but a lot of people will overlook this simple step.

If you're selling a product, you might not even want to always blatantly advertise that product. A lot of marketing is about brand awareness, and that's something vital for us to remember when creating our social media sites.

Like all social media, Facebook uses an algorithm to make sure that followers are only seeing the things that they absolutely want to. Facebook has blatantly stated that they put an emphasis on only making sure "meaningful content" was put on their users' news feeds. People get on Facebook to look at their college friends, their distant family members, and the person that their ex-boyfriend is dating. They don't get on there to shop, so it's up to you to make sure that this is what they end up doing. Give them a reason to click on your ad, then go to your page.

Facebook has recognized this themselves, which is why their algorithm tries to give people only the meaningful content that they want. If people aren't using Facebook, then they're not going to be making any money either, so the Facebook heads will want to make sure that the users are taken care of before the advertisers. Remember to use this algorithm to your advantage. The focus is going to be on creating a meaningful ad that brings value to your follower's lives.

Create the Ad

The ads that do the best on Facebook are ones that involve people. If you can include someone that is smiling or a group of diverse people, these are the things that are going to do the best. You get on Facebook to see people, so it will read well with your followers. Aside from that, Facebook will be less likely to weed out your posts as advertisements based on their algorithm if your post has people and looks natural.

Aside from that, videos are going to be very important for your brand strategy as well. Videos will be what stops a person as they're scrolling. They might not even know what your brand is at first, but if you come up with an ad that pulls them in, they'll stop. Once they've invested thirty seconds into a video, they'll be more likely to watch the rest of the thing.

Facebook is innovating the way you can share videos, too. You could share a simple video on your page, or you could choose to put your message into a story like you would on Instagram. You can also decide to do a live video, or perhaps you could try using their new TV methods as well. You should try to incorporate all of the tools that are offered so that you can determine which ones do the best.

Creating A Successful Ad Campaign

There are tools you can use on your own for Facebook marketing, but what's going to be the most helpful are the tools that exist within Facebook. All marketing campaigns start out with a trial period, at least, if they are trying to find a lot of success. What you will want to do is come up first with something that you think will be successful. From there, you will want to try it out and see if it does well or if it fails. This is the first and most natural step you can take to make sure that you are creating a successful ad campaign.

What's important to remember is that you should also only test out one ad campaign at a time. This way, you can make sure that you're getting accurate results when purchases are made. If you put ten different ads out there, you aren't going to know what works and what is hurting you. Facebook has its own analytics that will be important for you when measuring success as well. You can look at these analytics reports and see the type of people that are looking at your posts and interacting with your account.

Once you can determine what type of ad does the best, you can change what exists within the commercial and find the best way to sell your products to others. When an ad is successful, then you know you can depend on this to use in the future. What you also want to do, however, is make sure that you're coming up with ways of innovation, so the ad doesn't plateau and so that it stays relevant as well.

Target Audience

Targeting your audience has never been easier with Facebook ads. Facebook lets you decide when using paid advertisements, particular details about who you're going to be posting ads to. At first, you might think that getting your ad out to most people is the best method. Remember what we discussed on YouTube, however. If 10,000 people see your post, but only 100 of them are people in the demographics of the people that will benefit from your product or service the most, then you are only hurting your company. However, if you market your brand towards just 1,000 specific individuals, then you are more likely to have a more significant percentage of them interested, therefore getting a higher rate of return on purchases versus how many people might have viewed the ad.

You can use audience insights first to see who your type of followers is. It will tell you who might like an individual page, or who might be following a specific individual. This will help you in deciding if you are hitting the right demographic or if you need to find ways to reach further audiences.

After that, you can determine if you're going to target your audience based on categories or if you're going to do it with methods of shared interests. You can choose to market correctly to people that might have benefits in video game pages or certain types of other media. You could also sell to people that have recently been engaged, married, or expecting parents, based on their activity. It will be up to you, your business goals, and your advertising goals to determine what will do the best for your product.

Budget Allowed

To make sure that you are sticking to a budget, do plenty of organic marketing to find the methods that are the most successful. If you instead just start with paid ads, you're going to lose a lot of money. Make sure that you are only paying for ads that will result in getting paid as well. Brand awareness is essential, but make sure that you are still targeting towards people that are actually going to respond to your activity, not just trying to reach the most individuals as possible at once. If you are putting money towards making sure that you're getting directly paid, you're going to have a much higher return.

Determining the Type of Ad to Use

Once you've done a lot of testing and have looked at marketing results based on different statistics, you're going to have a better sense of what type of ad you should be using. There are some apparent indicators you can use when determining your ad type. If you're making instructional videos on YouTube, and that is your brand, then videos are the way to go. If you're a personality and want people to follow your brand, you might consider advertising your entire page rather than choosing just to sponsor one post.

You might also be a business that provides more one-time services, such as plumbing, electrical, and painting. Not many people will follow their electricians because they only need them a few times throughout their life, some people hopefully never. If this is your kind of business, then you might choose to simply advertise what you offer rather than trying to get people to follow you.

You should make sure that you're innovative with the type of ad that you're using as well. Just because you're using paid marketing doesn't mean that you should stop trying to use organic methods either. In fact, both will only help your Facebook page to grow.

Chapter 8:
Beating Facebook Algorithm for Explosive Growth

You don't always have to look for ways to be smarter than the algorithm. You have to look at how you can use it as your most excellent tool. The most important thing to remember when posting to Facebook is that you're sharing meaningful content. This is what Facebook has claimed it is trying to do with the new algorithm. There are some people that might think it's because they want to force businesses to pay for marketing rather than taking advantage of the organic methods, they can grow followers. Don't give into this. Instead, focus on making your content very natural, and something that doesn't get flagged as an ad. That will be the best way you can beat the Facebook algorithm.

Once you can make yourself first and foremost on many people's posts, then it will be a lot easier, in the end, to get them to consistently interact with you. Always remember that what works for your page might not work for someone else's, and vice versa.

Interact with Followers

Since Facebook has put an emphasis on creating content that is more meaningful, this includes posts that will have followers interacting with them. Get people talking about your posts. Ask questions, and start discussions. You might want to post a new picture of your merchandise and say something like, "Are you excited for what's coming to the store soon?" rather than making a simple comment announcing that you're adding new merchandise, you're starting a discussion. People might tag their friends, and others might even comment that they don't like it. Then there will be other individuals that will respond and say they do like it, and there you have it - a discussion! Facebook's algorithm will think that now this is more meaningful to users because people are talking on it, so they will put those posts in users' feeds where they can interact as well.

Interacting with your followers is a great way to make them feel better, as well. You can reply to their posts and like their pictures that might include your images or products. When you do this, you're satisfying your customers. At the same time, you're also making your page more meaningful, in Facebook's eyes as well.

Don't Use Engagement Bait

Avoid using what Facebook refers to as engagement bait. This will be anything that tells them to "like," "comment," or "share." If you post a video and tell people "click like and share with your friends! Make sure you subscribe on YouTube!" Facebook's algorithm will hide this from users. It will see the words: click, like, share, subscribe, and know that it is another business page's attempt at getting more action. Instead, look for organic ways you can start discussions.

Facebook weeds this out to make sure that their users aren't getting spammed with the kind of content that seems too advertorial. Instead, ask legitimate questions and get answers that will help grow your business and keep you involved with your followers. Rather than saying, "Tag a friend who would like this," say something like, "We all have that one friend who likes things like this. Who is yours?" They will then tag a friend, exposing you to even more users.

Use Facebook Groups

Creating groups is a great way to make sure that you're targeting a specific audience. You can decide to keep these groups exclusive and give those that are in it a sense that they are more in touch with your brand than your other followers. Then they will have a more exclusive interaction method that keeps them more loyal to your brand.

Creating an open group means more people will be able to connect with your brands and ideas that you're sharing within that. Just like we might follow people on Instagram as part of our identity, we often also look to the groups we're in as personal definitions. This can be true for individuals on Facebook, as well.

Post Only Original Content

Another way to make sure your content passes Facebook's algorithm is to make sure that it is entirely unique. If Facebook senses that an image is reposted or taken from someone else, then it might be flagged. Similarly, if your content is graphic or could violate any of their terms, it will have less of a chance of showing up on someone's feed as well.

If Facebook senses that you're sharing the same ad over and over again, then eventually you're going to get to a point where you show up as an advertiser. Unique content will also appeal to your followers more, giving them the sense that they can trust in you and your brand for individuality.

Don't Repost – Or Find New Ways to Use Old Content

A lot of companies will simply repost their old things to make sure that post gets a lot of likes. This was away some of your friends might have reached hundreds of likes on their profile picture as well. Facebook weeds out this kind of content.

Your followers are also going to want things that are new and unique. If you do repost something, make sure that it stands out from other postings. Don't just blatantly re-share it. Have a reason that you're deciding to repost something. Repost something old that got a lot of views, and maybe add it with the caption, "Who remembers this?" You're not only bringing back mature content that you know works but once again, you're getting your users involved and starting a discussion.

Videos Do Best

Videos do the best on Facebook. This is because when you have an eye-catching video, people will stop to watch. They will then invest time in you, and that will make them more likely to want to travel to your page or website.

When you share a video, it's more likely to get shared by your followers. They will enjoy having interesting content on their own feed. Your videos can also be shared among different platforms as well.

Videos are best because, on Instagram, you can have a snippet of a video and have the entire thing on Facebook, making it easier to encourage users to cross between your different social media pages.

Support Your Team

Since Facebook has an emphasis on creating meaningful content, then you'll want to make sure that you're posting things, including faces and real people. Your employees are going to be the best way to do this.

Your employees might not want to associate with their work on social media, and that should be acceptable. However, you can still encourage many of your staff to interact online and give them benefits to do so.

When companies can use their own employees, it makes your brand seem more personable and realistic. There will be a more significant emphasis on meaningful content, so it's going to be more likely to get shared as well.

Getting More Engagement Without Paying

You can shell out some money to make people come to your page through targeted ads. If you have it in your budget, paying to make sure your content not only reaches the people already following you, but other individuals not subscribed yet as well can be very helpful.

Unfortunately, it can also be pretty expensive. This is why we must be looking for all the ways that we can reach our followers without having to pay for it. When you're first getting started, your following is going to be a lot smaller, and you might not have the budget to pay for any marketing at all. Don't worry. You don't have to wait until you're consistently making money to reach out to new followers.

The current Facebook algorithm might seem scary, but really, we just need to look at ways that we're going to use this algorithm to our advantage. As we discussed, it's curated so that when users log onto Facebook, they are shown the things that give them the most meaning, the content that is closely related to the things that they like. We just have to make sure that your content is meaningful and eliciting engagement because this is what's going to keep people coming back to your page consistently.

We know now that you need to make sure that you're driving engagement. Some even have the theory that Facebook is trying to make more money by forcing businesses to pay for advertisements. Regardless of what everyone's true intentions are, we can't change the algorithm, so we have to look for ways that we can use it to our advantage.

The first thing that will help you increase engagement organically is to put an emphasis on timing. Just like with Instagram, Twitter, and YouTube, when you are posting, something is going to play a significant role in what attention your feed is getting. Luckily, Facebook actually has statistics they can give you based on your profile analytics so you can see what content does the best depending on a particular time. When you're first starting out, make sure you experiment with different times to understand what your followers will be the most likely to interact with.

Make your content all about your fans. We know, it can sound counterintuitive. You would think it should be all about you, right? Well, since Facebook wants to give meaningful content, this can mean that you need to share things explicitly curated to your followers.

Ensure that you are playing into trends and keeping up with pop culture. Something that works for users is to jump on the celebrity news and create entertaining content related to memes and trends that are currently getting the attention of followers. This is something that would work depending on your brand, however.

Even if your business isn't humorous, it's still a good tactic to use when trying to increase engagement. This is just another emotion that will help keep users more interested in consistently returning. Nothing ever just happens to "go viral." Make sure that you're looking at everything that does well and what doesn't.

Always make sure that your content is original. You never want to use stock photos, even though these exist on the Internet. Make sure your images are clear, never blurry, and aesthetically pleasing. Facebook isn't a place where aesthetics as an overall page matter, but you should still only share content that matches your brand.

Responding is an obvious way to drive engagement, but it's *when* you react that matters. People will typically expect a response within four hours of when you post. If your traffic is really flowing in and you have trouble responding, you could even try using a chatbot.

A lot of Facebook users will have different social media accounts, but since we know that this is the most used platform, a lot of people will probably only be on one account. This means you should focus on making content that's only for Facebook. Don't let this stop you from sharing things from other considerations as well.

Videos will do really well also, but you must be using Facebook videos. Facebook videos, including stories and live videos, will be more likely to show up in the feeds of your users than videos that have been shared from YouTube.

Keep your content simple, and don't post as frequently as you might assume you should. In fact, some brands find that their content does the best and is the most likely to get shared when they only post once a day. If you're putting the effort in, you'll notice the traffic increasing.

Share interesting information. People will like to share informative content. It makes them seem more intelligent and as if they are the ones that have something valuable to offer to their Facebook friends as well. For example, if you're a clothing brand, you might share exciting information about the materials used in your clothes, and some scientific data on those materials. People love engaging with "fun facts."

Whatever you do, don't minimize the effort you're putting in. No matter how hard you might feel like you're working, there's likely someone working twice as hard as you out there, or at least we should assume so.

Chapter 9:
The Last Piece of Your Marketing Empire Twitter

Twitter is not a social media platform that should be forgotten about. It does have far fewer users than the other three social media platforms we discussed throughout this book. Still, with over three hundred million users, Twitter is very much relevant and should be considered just as much as the others. There are plenty of users that are on Twitter that won't show up on Instagram or Facebook. There are also going to be users that don't necessarily want to follow you on Instagram, or like you on Facebook, but they might just end up following you on Twitter.

It is in some ways more casual, and for other users, taken more seriously. There are certain people that will use Twitter for fun and Instagram professionally, and vice versa on the different platforms as well. The more we can include both of them, and all the social media platforms in general, the more return we're going to discover from our social media marketing efforts.

Why Twitter Is Just as Important as Facebook And YouTube

Facebook and YouTube have over a billion users, and Instagram is well on its way to reaching numbers this shockingly high as well. For Twitter to get to a billion users, it would just about half to double. However, something is going on with Twitter that we really need to remember. The site will have close to a half a million people enter or view the place that doesn't even use Twitter accounts each and every month. These people might be users that aren't logged in, but they are also individuals that don't want to make their own Twitter portfolio. Even though you might not have access to as many users as you would on Facebook, YouTube, or Instagram, you still have exposure to billions of sets of eyes a year, being confident that people both on and off Twitter can see your Twitter advertisements.

How It Works

On Twitter, there are over half a million new tweets that are sent each and every day. This equals to be a few thousand per second. Though it's not a billion minutes of YouTube watched, that's still a ton of content that is being shared throughout different pages and among various accounts. If that isn't enough for you to jump on the Twitter bandwagon, then what is!

When it comes to what you can tweet, it's very similar as it would be on other sites. You can post a picture, a video, or a simple comment. You can retweet other people, which means that you're posting their words on your own. You can also favorite people's likes, and these will go into a collection of your liked tweets. You can choose to share this information with others, or you can make the tweets that you like, as well as the people that you follow, private.

Most social media work in the same way. You get online, you post something, and people react to that post. What differs in between is who is on that site, and what kind of content you're most likely to post. YouTube, you're most likely going to post a video. Instagram, a picture. Twitter, you're probably going to display text, whether it's your own words or quote, or a link to an article.

Facebook is sort of a combination of all of those things. You can post your Tweets to your Facebook just as quickly as you could post your Instagram pictures there as well. When you use all three of these and then Facebook to keep them all connected as well, you're going to find the most success for your brand.

High-Quality Content

While all social media aims to have high-quality content, your Twitter is going to need that as well. This is because you want something that will be retweeted. You will get a lot of benefits from your own personal followers, but you want to ensure that they're sharing your profile and necessary information with others as well.

High-quality content should be something that informs users. Many Twitter accounts exist so that they can follow trending news and the latest hot topics. Make sure that your tweets are staying relevant by paying attention to trends, and the hashtags that are getting the most popular on Twitter.

Remember that high quality doesn't equate to seriousness. While a lot of people will get their news and essential information from Twitter, many individuals will also go there merely for jokes and comedy. It's up to you to make sure that you are posting shareable content that gets likes and attention from others, just as you would on other social media sites.

At the same time, people also respond to ads more on Twitter and are less likely to feel as though they are being spammed by different companies. A method you can use to grow your followers before we even get into hacking the algorithm includes using automated tweets, and automated follows. This will allow you to stay relevant and consistent without having to worry about always being on your phone and posting more. If you automatically follow new people, then there is a chance that those people will follow you back, and you put in almost no effort to do this.

Chapter 10:
Twitter Algorithm for Massive Engagement

Twitter's Algorithm is similar to all the others we discussed throughout the book. It merely wants to give its followers the content that they want. When social media started, it was meant for sharing and communication, and then from there, people began to use it as a marketing tool. Many users became upset with just how many ads they would see, and it caused a dip in social media, Facebook taking the hardest hit. Since social media creators learned their lesson, there has been an emphasis on making sure blatant advertisements that aren't paid for to stay out of the feed of users' profiles. What we need to do now is make sure that our content is just as personable as everyone else's posts.

While followers don't have to pay anything to use the app, they are the most essential part of Twitter. If everyone quit Twitter, there wouldn't be money lost from membership fees like how Netflix or Hulu would suffer. The money lost would be from advertisers. Though you are the one that controls the money, the customers and followers are the ones that decide what is done with that money. We have to make sure we are satisfying their needs and giving them the quality content that they are so hungry for.

Twitter users can see both what people posted as their top tweets and which ones were posted most recently. This is great because it gives you the chance to reach out twice. On Instagram, you'll have to be focused on making sure your content is personally relevant to your followers to get it to show up in their feed. Twitter still allows options for users so they can see what was posted the most recently.

There is also an ICYMI section for users to see top tweets they missed the first time. Not only could you get Twitter to participate in your marketing tactics through organic posting and them seeing it around the time the tweet was sent. You can also make sure that they understand your marketing again through the top tweets or an ICYMI section. (ICYMI = in case you missed it)

Happening Now will feature things that are from more than just followers. This will be similar to an Instagram explore page, having things that are being talked about, shared, retweeted, and liked the most. This will also give your brand a chance to stick out if you manage to come up with a viral-worthy tweet.

Trends for You is just what it sounds like: trends, popular hashtags, and things that are making the news. You might not always be able to make the top stories, but you could start a potentially explosive hashtag and find popularity and relevance through that method.

Posting

This is another method that differs among the various social media platforms. You'll want to make sure that you're posting often enough for tweets to be seen, but not too much to where you're spamming followers. You are going to want to tweet at least three times a day to start and make sure that you do so at different times as well. Twitter is where you're going to want to make sure that you are posting at the right time more than any other social media platform. You'll also have to do your best to ensure that you are posting more frequently than other sites as well.

Twitter users are generally following more people than other sites, and most people will tweet several times a day, meaning that your followers will have a lot of content that they have to sift through. While it might seem like a lot to post, remember that not every post has to be organic. The three pillars that you make in a day should certainly be things that differ, but you could use similar pictures, or retweet old stuff to keep older content relevant and newer content active.

Twitter is like YouTube in that a lot is consumed at once and throughout different ways. You want to make sure that you are keeping your presence active. If people feel as though they can't rely on you for new tweets and content that is consistently fresh, then they will follow and move onto another brand.

This is all-important for the Twitter algorithm. On Facebook, if you don't post as often, it might prioritize your postings, but only if that person already has interaction with your brand. On Twitter, if you don't tweet that much, there won't be as much of a priority, because there is a higher demand for relevant and essential content. The more you tweet, the more likely you are to get a like or a retweet, which means the more likely you are to gain followers and attention. Though what Facebook and Twitter's algorithm aims to do is the same (show users' meaningful content), how they decide to use an algorithm to achieve this is going to be different.

Use Twitter Analytics

While we may have a lot of tips packed into this book, the most essential information for growing your Twitter presence exists within your own account. Twitter provides analytics not just to business profiles, but to everyone! You can see how many people saw your tweet and keep track of the activity that happens around your tweet. This is a great way to check what is working the best and what can be improved on within your own account.

Most social media sites will have these algorithms, but it's the most important for Twitter. You are likely going to be putting the most amount of content out only in terms of how many posts you might be making. What exists within those posts might not be as relevant, but you will still be a little more active if you are on Twitter. This means that you are going to have to weed out a lot of more bad posts than you would on Instagram, and Twitter analytics are going to be very important in helping you decide what is right and what is wrong.

Emphasizing Top Tweets

Once you post something on Instagram, it will stay relevant for about a week, maybe still showing up on some people explore pages. After a month or so, that picture will likely get buried in with the rest, and people will have moved on to the next Instagram posts. The same can be said about Facebook. Where Twitter and YouTube connect, however, is in that both older YouTube videos and older Tweets can have a way of coming back around and staying relevant.

You can pin specific tweets to your page. This might be an essential tweet, such as an announcement about a new product, or an update on your services. It could also only be something for brand emphasizing, like a joke that you thought was really funny, or your tweet that got retweeted by a celebrity. Whatever it may be, it's a way to let our followers be reminded of the things that we already said.

To keep old content fresh and find ways to reuse what has already worked, look for ways that you can promote your tweets. You might do this by retweeting your own retweets and thinking of creative ways to "tweet" yourself. For example, if you are a business owner that happens to own an art gallery, you might post a tweet about the opening of a show with a stunning picture of a piece that's in the show.

Then, when it's getting towards the end of the month and the exhibit is coming to a close, you'll want to send a tweet to remind people not to miss the show. If you send a regular tweet, like "Get tickets while you can!" people might overlook this, as they likely see that a few times throughout their feeds depending on who they follow. What you could do instead, however, is go back to that original tweet that you shared for the initial opening announcement. You could then retweet that, and say something like, "Who hasn't seen this piece yet? There are only a few more days to come check it out!"

This is a way of marketing that feels more natural. It brings people back to something they've already seen, something they're familiar with. It works for the Twitter algorithm as well because that first tweet might have gotten a lot of attention, meaning the retweet could get just as much notice as well. Finally, it's helpful because it's going to sell something to your followers without feeling too much like an advertisement. It gives them the push they need to buy tickets without feeling like they are being sold something. Though you might not own an art gallery, you can still use this same form of "retweeting" or "tweeting at" yourself that was used in this example.

The Twitter Growth Hack
Twitter still has hundreds of millions of users, even though it seems like it's not the top social media site. Each and every day, hundreds of thousands of new tweets are sent all day, nonstop. The only reason

someone isn't tweeting at any given time would be if there were a Twitter shutdown.

Even if the power went out in one area, there are still plenty of other places that Twitter users will be consistently active in. Even in China, where Twitter is blocked, there are still ten million active users. 9/10 political leaders use Twitter, and almost 4 out of 10 millennials are on Twitter. As a marketer, you should know that millennials are the group that will be most likely to buy your product, and they are the most successful demographic to market towards.

The thing about Twitter is that a lot of people will screenshot tweets and even post them to other sites. Though you might not be on Twitter yet, or there might be other users that aren't as active on Twitter, you should still ensure that you are including this into your content marketing strategy.

Even if you haven't been on Twitter, you've seen a tweet, because many people will share these on other social media sites. Twitter is great because it isn't as focused on Instagram when it comes to making your personal brand and aesthetic. You will still have to ensure that you're keeping up with an overall look that will keep people interested in your brand, but you can also feel satisfied knowing that there won't be as much pressure to keep up appearances on Twitter.

Twitter has many international users as well, which will help you with your global outreach strategies. Not only is this an app that keeps you connected to the people in your area, but you will also have access to the hundreds of millions of other users that get on daily across the globe. Never before have we been able to breach the walls of communication so easily. You can send a tweet to someone across the country all within just a few seconds.

Twitter has the highest reach out of all the platforms. Though there are fewer users, there is a much higher chance that you are going to be able to reach one of your followers organically rather than having to pay to have your tweet promoted. This means that you can implement different methods of marketing and try out new things with more freedom than you would have on sites like Facebook and Instagram.

When we can put an emphasis on merely interacting and reaching your followers rather than having the pressure of looking the best and being the most engaging, it will give you the freedom needed to really find the things that work for your client base, solidifying your brand.

The best amount to tweet is 8-10 times each and every day. This can seem like a lot, even for a user that is on their personality. Now, if you have a particular brand, you might not want to post as frequently, especially if your content isn't relevant. You can simply try posting one tweet a day and see if this is enough to get people interested. However, you should still be retweeting other people and liking content. Ultimately, it will be up to you to evaluate your brand and really determine what the right number of tweets per day should be sent.

Staying active is going to keep people more interested in your content. This doesn't mean just tweeting either. Get online and respond to the tweets that other people are sending to you and tagging you in. You should be interacting with other people as well. Make sure that you curate who you are following to people that are relevant to your brand and overall image. Though it might be tempting to load your following list with people that interest you the most on a personal level, you should try to keep that to your own page. Instead, focus on brands that inspire you and encourage you, ones that are successful and offer innovative ideas. If you can do this, then you will have a list of people that you can interact with that might help expose you to even larger audiences that are similar to the one that you've already curated for your own brand.

The hard part can be that each and every tweet has to have meaning. Even if you are simply responding to someone, you don't want to have everyone be just the "thumbs up" emoji, or a "halacha." You want to create content with meaning and keep messages clear and straightforward when you are tweeting. You should always make sure that each of your own tweets is something that would look good if it appeared on another person's page.

At the same time, you have to ensure that you are making new replies as well. Keep your responses a little more casual than you would the specific single tweets you share on your own profile, but you still want to ensure that you're keeping it interesting and professional. If you're flooding your follower's feed with meaningless content, they won't want to remain subscribed to you and instead will look elsewhere for their entertainment and premium content.

Share an inspirational quote or a meaningful message. These can be great ways to bring brand awareness. Even if it's a quote from someone you like but not necessarily one that you thought of on your own, then it can help you to curate your brand and give people something to share with their followers.

Some studies have shown that doing a follow/unfollow method is going to help out in increasing followers, but not necessarily engagement. In the beginning, if you're starting from scratch, then this can be a way to launch yourself off the ground. You can follow a few hundred pages a day, so you can start to follow brands that matter to you, their followers, and other people that seem as though they would have an interest in you.

Follow as many people as you want, and once you've created a particular audience, you can limit the people that you're following. Anyone that isn't following back you can unfollow, and those that have subscribed you can interact with to help build their interest in your brand. This should only be a short-term solution, however, because brands like this can seem spammy.

Mentions are another vital part of growing your following. These could help you reach out to your followers and help drive engagement towards your page.

When it comes to when to Tweet, you'll want to hit all of the sweet spots. These will be the same as Instagram – morning, lunch, after work, after dinner. You can also try and find new times that work well for Twitter because you will have more leniency with how often you can post things. You might find that tweeting late at night really works best for your brand, or that your followers are more of the morning kind.

Look at Twitter as a vessel to your other social media platforms. Since you should be tweeting more often than you would post on Facebook or Instagram, then you have the opportunity to reference your other social media sites and drive traffic there. People are going to be more likely to follow users on Twitter because it's a more easily consumable, quicker platform than Facebook or Instagram.

This will give you the chance to reach out to them and tweet things like, "check out my new Instagram post," or "see the Facebook video going live in 5 minutes." You will want to think of your own message but remember that Twitter will help increase awareness to the other sites, making it easier to connect them all.

You should try to retweet your old content as well, as this can help engage more people too. Sometimes, we might send one tweet out, and it gets a ton of likes and retweets, only for the next one to get hardly any attention at all.

When you're struggling to come up with several tweets a day, you can go back to older things and bring it around again. You could try again with things that didn't do well and see if a different time could bring it more successful. You could also put a focus on the things that already did well, knowing that there's a chance it could get retweeted even more.

Ensure that you are keeping your profile up to date and interesting to look at as well. Though you don't need to have a perfectly matching aesthetic, you should still do your best to make sure you're providing valuable information that others will find use from. At the same time, you can also take this moment to tell more about yourself and even share a funny joke or comment that will keep people interested.

Choose one tweet that seems to have done better than the rest, and make sure that you are pinning this. Twitter has the opportunity for you to post something at the top of your feed that will help give followers a little insight into what it is that you're trying to do on your Twitter account.

Pick a tweet that got the most attention or one that's making an exciting new announcement. You can change this pinned tweet out as well, so sometimes you can post exciting news, and other times, you can keep it updated with announcements of the month.

Share content that you've seen on the web. Say something about an article that relates to your brand. Even if it's not something that will completely promote your brand, a new trending article or controversial topic can get people talking. For example, maybe you're a beauty product brand that includes essential oils in their products.

If you stumble upon an article praising the benefits of essential oil, then you can share this on your Twitter and get people talking about it so that they are sharing your page and retweeting you while also engaging with others.

The number one growth hack, however, is engagement. Yep, just like the rest of the platforms, you need to engage on Twitter as well. The thing about Twitter is that it's all about engagement. Facebook is all about connecting with others, Instagram sharing beautiful pictures, YouTube videos, and so on for other platforms not mentioned.

On Twitter, you're supposed to share text posts, thoughts, and ideas that are important to you and your brand. The best way to get attention to your site is to use it for the purposes it was intended for in the first place.

Do a Q and A! If you open your Twitter up to have people ask you questions and you give them answers, this is going to be an excellent way for you to encourage engagement. You are providing your viewers and followers the chance to get some thoughts and ideas out about your brand they might have been holding in, and you can inform new followers and others that aren't already subscribed about who you are.

You can pick and choose which questions you want to use as well. To do this, simply state that you will be doing a Q and A. Then, people will start to reply and tweet at you asking questions. You can answer them right on Twitter, or you can make them go to your other social media, saying you're going to answer them on Instagram or in a Facebook video.

It's All About Interacting

Just like with Instagram, Facebook, and YouTube, interacting is going to be very important. What's different about Twitter is that there isn't a comment section, but rather, replies to your tweets. This means that your comments are more likely going to be seen by others and their followers than the comments you might share on a particular Facebook post.

Many people will admit that they are more likely to buy into a brand or fall for their marketing tactics when they have interacted with that brand through Twitter. This is very important for business owners to remember. Simply favoriting someone's tweet could be enough to show them that you really care about their business, and they'll end up coming back more likely than if you had ignored their tweets.

Interacting also gives you a great way to deal with dissatisfied customers. If someone is unhappy with your product or service, they might choose to take to Twitter to voice their opinion. From there, you can respond to them professionally and get to a place where they are happy. While doing this, your followers, as well as their followers, will also see the interaction (depending on their algorithms), and it will help to expose your brand. The other person's followers can see that you are professional and that they can trust you to do business.

Twitter polls are another great way that you can interact with your followers. The great thing about elections is also that it is free marketing! To see if someone liked your product, you used to have to hire someone to mediate a research study and find willing participants to do so for free or for a small fee. Now, you can tweet, "Do you like our new product?" and people will be willing to answer!

You can get them interacting, spreading awareness about your brand, and expose yourself to people that don't even follow you. Many Twitter users will love merely answering a question also if they never heard of you or your brand. All while you are doing this, you are tracking important information about your brand or product that will help you improve it for the better simply based on your customer's wants and needs.

The more you interact with your followers, the more likely you will be to pop up into their feed according to Twitter's algorithms. Not only will this method help expose you to your followers more, but it will help them show your appreciation to them as customers rather than just your followers.

Chapter 11:
How to Monetize Your Social Media Following

Once you've gained a following, your new mission is to make more money from that. As a company, you should know that brand exposure and making more profit is never a bad thing. It can be harder the more money you make, but it is always worth it. At first, it was all about making sure that you could grow a following in the first place to get people to buy into your brand or product. Whether you wanted to attract new customers for your products, or you're a social media influencer that wants attention from advertisers to make money from sponsorships, getting a following was the hard part. Some people might seemingly try everything and still never get over 1,000 followers, so if you managed to get the right amount of people subscribed, you should feel very accomplished and proud.

Now, it's time to actually make a profit from that following! You got them there in the first place, and with their following also came the fact that they might have made a purchase or monetary subscription right off the bat. Now, you have to find ways to make those who haven't become customers yet people that are going to buy into your brand and ensure the ones that already have been taken care of, helping you to keep growing more.

Combine All Platforms

If you're not doing it already, you should find ways to include all of your social media apps in the bios of your other apps. Your Twitter should have a link to your Instagram, and your YouTube should have a link to your Facebook. Wherever you are on these apps, encourage your followers to visit these other platforms. By doing this, you are creating brand awareness and helping to make your followers more loyal to you, following you on different accounts.

If you manage to keep all of your different platforms together, it is easier for people to find you as well. Make sure that you are also constantly reminding people to visit these other pages because new users might not realize at first that you are on more than one platform, even if it is something that you put in your bio.

Rather than sharing content on all of these platforms, decide where to accurately put certain things. This way, you can help encourage your followers to visit these other sites. For example, if you put out a new video on YouTube, instead of sharing that video on Instagram as well, just share a snippet. Then, they will go to YouTube to see the video. When you do this, two things will happen. You are getting more ad revenue should you have monetized videos that make you money from merely being watched. You will also have a higher chance of gaining a new follower on this platform. If someone that follows you on Instagram goes to your YouTube to watch a video you teased, they are more likely to subscribe to your YouTube channel, especially if they're already logged in.

Strategies to Make Your Followers Customers

One surefire way to gain more customers from your followers is to talk about your products – don't just try to sell them. People are more likely to turn into customers when they feel as though they are following an authentic person. If they get the idea that they are being sold something, or that a specific brand is trying to trick them into spending money, then they are more likely to feel as though they are just another customer. Your followers don't want to be customers. They want to be followers. They don't want to have to go through loops to get your product, and they don't want to be force-fed media and products.

To get people to your website and buying your products, you have to connect with the customers. They want to be able to interact with you, and they want to know that their voice is heard. Your followers want to see your product being used by people they know, and they want exclusive offers. However, you can make your social media use friendlier and more personal to your followers, then the easier it will be to have them turning into customers. If you can share your brand genuinely, you will be able to win over the people that followed you in the first place. Some people don't want to spend money at all, but when they feel like they can trust you and your brand, will be more willing to make a purchase they might have otherwise forgotten about, should it have been a less personal brand. Aside from being private and reaching out to them, these next few sections are going to cover a few more ways that you can turn your followers into loyal customers.

Give Away Freebies

It seems counterintuitive to give away something free to make money, but it can actually be the way that you make money in the end. Not only will you have people more willing to try your product, but you can also get them to fall in love with your brand. Freebies don't just have to be products either. They can be more pictures, podcasts, or videos that you only share through a monetized platform like Patron. By finding a way to offer these goods, services, and forms of content for free, you will grow your following and have them subscribe to you more often to create loyal customers.

For example, if you are a comedian trying to brand yourself, you might have a YouTube series that people have to pay for to view. If you give away the first episode for free, it might end up causing the people to pay for the rest of the series more frequently than if they would have had to pay for the first episode initially. You are, at the very least, exposing your brand and gaining awareness, making people more likely to go back to that show as well, buying later or consistently checking back to see if it had become free.

There are different ways that you can send out freebies too. You can simply give a product away, such as a lotion that you're selling, or even a book you wrote. You could give it to all of your followers, or you could select fifty people that you've encouraged to "like" or "subscribe." People love getting free stuff, so you can make them happy with that by also gaining a following for yourself.

People that get your free product might just use it and move onto the next thing. However, there will be many people that like your product and end up buying more of it, even though they wouldn't have paid for it initially.

Offer Follower-Only Deals

Another great way to keep your followers loyal is to give them deals that only they can access. You can tell them that you're going to send a code through messenger, or just simply make your account temporarily private and give away a discount code for your website, or a different free service. By exclusively letting your followers know that only they have access to this freebie or discount, they will become more loyal to you because they feel as though you're being more loyal to them.

Thank Your Customers After They Buy

We've been told the importance of saying thank you and showing gratitude since we were old enough to talk. Making someone feel appreciated is the quickest way to get them to like you. As a brand, it can be easy to expect our customers to simply keep buying into us after they have already made a purchase. What we have to remember, however, is that follow-up satisfaction checks are just as necessary as initial interactions, because we could still lose a customer if they are not happy. Rather than assuming once a customer, a customer for life, make sure that those that have already given you money are happy instead of putting all your focus on new people that will provide you with even more money.

One great way to say thank you is to do so through your packaging, or a message after they've used your service. You can find ways to show appreciation on Facebook as well! When someone tags your product, or only you, in one of their posts, reach out and acknowledge that post. Perhaps they're wearing a dress from your clothing company and tagged you in the pic. Make sure to at least like it to let them know that you are grateful for their free advertisement! When someone mentions you in their story, Instagram even allows you to post that in your own account, so you can show appreciation through this way as well. The options you have for showing your customers that you are happy they are there are really endless.

Achieving Financial Freedom

The point of starting your brand in the first place might have been something more significant than making money. You might have wanted to simply spread awareness as a social media influencer, or perhaps you wanted to offer a quality product against all the other unsatisfactory brands that exist. No matter what your intention was in the first place, as you grow your social media, it's essential to make sure that you are going in a path towards financial freedom. There are many reasons why freeing from yourself from money can be so important, but we don't need to tell you all the bases.

First and foremost, when you've grown your success on social media and found wealth, you have freed yourself from all the stress that comes along with wanting and needing money. After that relief, you can realize that your brand can grow to its fullest potential once you've reached financial freedom as well. If you don't have to worry about making money as much as you did in the first place, you start to have room to experience with your brand more. When you do this, you can discover new things about your company that might have gone unnoticed had you stuck to the same brands.

Obviously, having a large following is your first step towards financial freedom achieved through social media marketing. What we've already read throughout the book went over that, so in the last few sections of this chapter, we're going to give you more ways you can profit off your large following other than just driving website traffic and product sales.

Host Events

A great way to not only make money but to spread even more brand awareness is to host an event. When you do this, you are getting people excited about your brand and helping them to spread the word. You can host an event in whatever category suits your brand. For example, if you're a guitar company, you might host a concert, or maybe an album release of a local band. If your company is one that offers resume writing services, then you might host a workshop on how to create a cover letter or how to nail an interview. If you're a social media influencer, you could simply host your own birthday or different holiday party at a local bar or venue. The options are endless, but it's essential to know that you have options with this marketing tactic.

You can charge admission to these events, have suggested donations, or find a different company to help sponsor the game as well. There are many different ways you can choose to host a game, but it's essential to know that you can make money from this method. You can invite people on Facebook and post pictures to Instagram and Twitter. You could create a YouTube video around the event and share it on other platforms as well. People can say that they are interested in the event on Facebook, and they might even tag their friends. You will be able to make money from the game itself while also profiting from brand awareness and exposure to your different social media pages.

Creating Merch

There are reasons people liked your page or followed you in the first place. There's also a reason that they will like and share your pictures, videos, and posts. By loving your products and buying into your brand, your followers are including you in part of their identity. No matter how big or how small, your brand has an influence on them, which is why they choose to stay dedicated to you on social media.

When you become aware of this, you will realize that you can profit from yourself or your company through merchandise. People follow you on social media, and they like your posts, letting their followers know that they support you. Many people will want to show this by buying your merchandise as well. You can create t-shirts, coffee cups, pictures, pillows, calendars, and many more forms of merchandise that include your logos or your images. If you can find a funny twist or aesthetically pleasing design that provides for your brand, this will be even better. When you can achieve this, then you can start to make money on your name alone.

Creating a Product

If you don't have a product in the first place, you could potentially create one so that you are making even more money initially. Not only will you have found success from being an influencer or someone that provides a service online, but you could also expand your wealth and make more money from merely selling different goods and products. It can be a single product as well, so if it doesn't do that great, then you don't have to keep selling it. It is just another project you can try that could grow your brand. Who knows, you could end up coming up with the most excellent new product!

The important thing is to simply remember relevancy. What could your followers gain from your product that is similar to why they followed you in the first place, while still providing something new enough that they would spend more money on you. If you are a social media influencer that creates exercise videos, you could sell your followers a pair of workout pants. If you are a freelance makeup artist, you could sell your own lipstick! There are many options that you have as any form of brand, and it's up to you to get creative and think of a product that will make your customers even more loyal to you than they already are.

Write a Book

Writing a book can be an excellent way for many different brands and companies to make even more money. The great thing about books is that they are also passive forms of income. Years after you've published a book, you might still be making money from it. Anyone can be an author, and with the right editor, your words can really positively influence someone no matter how little experience you might have.

Just like with thinking of a product, it's only essential that you are writing a book about something relevant. If you are a real estate agent and write a cookbook on a ketogenic diet, you might not get much attention for your book, and it wouldn't really be helping your real estate business grow. Instead, you might write a book on how to buy a house, or how to become a real estate investor.

Selling your book will help you make more money from the followers you already have. It will also make them more loyal by allowing you to get even more personal with them. Books are your follower's way to put themselves in your head and be influenced by your words. It will make it much easier for you to have an influence on them outside the book after they've read it as well.

Chapter 12:
Social Media Marketing is the Future

If you haven't realized this already, we can only plan for futures that are going to be filled with social media. Unless there's some apocalyptic sort of incident that wipes out the Internet, we can be sure that we will be using Facebook, Instagram, YouTube, and other forms of social media for decades to come.

There are specific individuals that don't like this idea. Some people would rather stay away from the Internet and focus on the real world. While times might have seemed simpler in some ways before social media, they are improved in many ways in other forms, and we might not always see those advantages initially.

It's more critical for you to get online and share your brand's views and images now more than ever. Each second, you're not online is a missed opportunity to expose your mission statement. When you are depriving your company of social media, you are taking the chance away to go to the next step.

You can find success for your company without social media, that's for sure. You could easily make money from old-fashioned ways and never use social media. You don't have to use it to find success. What you need to remember, however, is that it will always help you find more success. If you can make a significant amount of money and grow a large following without using these free online platforms, imagine how much more you can expand your image when you expand your audience to hundreds of thousands of people.

Social media is the present, and it's absolutely the future as well. Many brands already are only marketing through social media, and others are going towards that direction at a rapid rate. The numbers already show that your competitors are on these sites, so it's time for you to make sure that you are putting yourself out there as well.

The Importance of This Marketing

Social media isn't just a new way to market your brand. It's transformed the way that we market ourselves as a society in general. It's not only brands that are trying to gain regular capital. People are using social media as a way to increase social capital. How many followers one has might indicate where they are at in particular social standing in their life.

People take social media very seriously, and there is an emphasis on having the best and most followed account. Though it might not be that important to you on a personal level, you must see how powerful it will be for your brand. When we use this massive tool to our advantage, we will quickly find the boost we need for our brand to elevate the stakes. You could double, triple, or even quadruple the number of customers you have if you just find the right methods to market yourself online.

It can seem overwhelming at first, but always remember that there will be trial and error periods throughout your social media marketing journey. Just because your first YouTube video doesn't hit 1,000 views doesn't mean that your fourth or fifth can't hit 1,000,000. Though it might feel like a lottery at some points, remember that there's a lot more involved than just chance. You can hit the jackpot if you are smart, dedicated, and willing to persevere.

If you find this book helpful in any way a review to support my endeavors is much appreciated.

Value Branding with Social Media Marketing

Casey Greenwood

www.ingramcontent.com/pod-product-compliance
Lightning Source LLC
Chambersburg PA
CBHW030526210326
41597CB00013B/1046